Dialogue Activities

Cambridge Handbooks for Language Teachers

This is a series of practical guides for teachers of English and other languages. Illustrative examples are usually drawn from the field of English as a foreign or second language, but the ideas and techniques described can equally well be used in the teaching of any language.

Recent titles in this series:

Teaching English Spelling
A practical guide
RUTH SHEMESH *and* SHEILA WALLER

Personalizing Language Learning
Personalized language learning activities
GRIFF GRIFFITHS *and* KATHRYN KEOHANE

Teach Business English
A comprehensive introduction to Business English
SYLVIE DONNA

Learner Autonomy
A guide to activities which encourage learner responsibility
ÁGOTA SCHARLE *and* ANITA SZABÓ

The Internet and the Language Classroom (second edition)
Practical classroom activities and projects
GAVIN DUDENEY

Planning Lessons and Courses
Designing sequences of work for the language classroom
TESSA WOODWARD

Learner English (second edition)
MICHAEL SWAN *and* BERNARD SMITH

Teaching Large Multilevel Classes
NATALIE HESS

Writing Simple Poems
Pattern poetry for language acquisition
VICKI L. HOLMES *and* MARGARET R. MOULTON

Laughing Matters
Humour in the language classroom
PÉTER MEDGYES

Using Authentic Video in the Language Classroom
JANE SHERMAN

Stories
Narrative activities for the language classroom
RUTH WAJNRYB

Language Activities for Teenagers
edited by SETH LINDSTROMBERG

Pronunciation Practice Activities
A resource book for teaching English pronunciation
MARTIN HEWINGS

Five-Minute Activities for Business English
PAUL EMMERSON *and* NICK HAMILTON

Games for Language Learning (third edition)
ANDREW WRIGHT, DAVID BETTERIDGE *and* MICHAEL BICKBY

Drama Techniques (third edition)
A resource book of communication activities for language teachers
ALAN MALEY *and* ALAN DUFF

Dictionary Activities
CINDY LEANEY

Five-Minute Activities for Young Learners
PENNY McKAY *and* JENNI GUSE

Dialogue Activities

Exploring spoken interaction in the language class

Nick Bilbrough

CAMBRIDGE UNIVERSITY PRESS
Cambridge, New York, Melbourne, Madrid, Cape Town, Singapore, São Paulo

Cambridge University Press
The Edinburgh Building, Cambridge CB2 8RU, UK

www.cambridge.org
Information on this title: www.cambridge.org/9780521689519

First published 2007

Printed in the United Kingdom at the University Press, Cambridge

A catalogue record for this publication is available from the British Library

Library of Congress Cataloging in Publication data
Bilbrough, Nick.
Dialogue activities: exploring spoken interaction in the language class / Nick Bilbrough.
p. cm. – (Cambridge handbooks for language teachers)
Includes bibliographical references and index.
ISBN 978-0-521-68951-9 (pbk.)
1. English language–Study and teaching–Foreign speakers. 2. English language–Spoken English–Study and teaching. I. Title. II. Series.

PE1128.A2B475 2007
428'.0071–dc22

2007001839

ISBN 978-0-521-68951-9 paperback

Contents

Thanks and acknowledgements

Most books are a dialogue. This has been one more than most. From our initial discussion over fish and chips in a pub in Camden Town, through a long series of emailed exchanges, I am indebted to Scott Thornbury for his experience, insightful comments and unfailing enthusiasm for the project. Thanks too to Frances Amrani, Laila Friese and Michelle Simpson at CUP for editorial guidance.

I am especially grateful to students and staff at both the Brasshouse Language Centre, Birmingham and International House Santiago for trialing ideas and inspiring new ones, and to Emma, Andre and Charlie for all the misspent weekends.

The authors and publishers are grateful to the following for permission to reproduce copyright material. While every effort has been made, it has not always been possible to identify the sources of all the material used, or to contact the copyright holders. If any omissions are brought to our notice, we will be happy to include the appropriate acknowledgements on reprinting.

This publication has made use of the Cambridge and Nottingham Corpus of Discourse in English (CANCODE). CANCODE is a five-million word computerised corpus of spoken English, made up of recordings from a variety of settings in the countries of the United Kingdom and Ireland. The corpus is designed with a substantial organised database giving information on participants, settings and conversational goals. CANCODE was built by Cambridge University Press and the University of Nottingham and it forms part of the Cambridge International Corpus (CIC). It provides insights into language use, and offers a resource to supplement what is already known about English from other, non-corpus-based research, thereby providing valuable and accurate information for researchers and those preparing teaching materials. Sole copyright of the corpus resides with Cambridge University Press, from whom all permission to reproduce material must be obtained.

Texts

pp. 3-4: Extract 'Asking for change' taken from *Situational Dialogues* by Michael Ockenden. © 1972, p. 41 and p. 79: adapted tape scripts taken from *Wavelength Elementary* by Kathy Burke and Julia Brooks. © 1999. Used by permission of Pearson Education Limited; p. 4: Extract 'At the hairdressers' taken from *Departures* by Bernard Hartley and Peter Viney. © Oxford University Press 1978; p. 5: Extract 'At the hairdressers' taken from *Exploring Spoken English* by Ronald Carter and Michael McCarthy. © 1997, p. 8: Extract 'Burns contractor' taken from *Simulations Language Teaching* by Ken Jones. © 1982, p. 23: Extract 'Dangerous Pastimes' taken from *Language in Use Upper-Intermediate Classroom book* by Adrian Doff and Christopher Jones. © 1997, p. 36: Extract 'Every morning' taken from *Help* by Philip Prowse. © 1999, p. 64: Extract 'What do you do?' taken from *Language in Use Beginner Classroom book* by Adrian Doff and Christopher Jones. © 1999, p. 66: Extract 'dialogue between Gary and Rosa' taken from *Messages 3 Teachers'*

Resource Book by Meredith Levy and Diane Goodey. © 2006, p. 70: 'Tape script review 3' taken from *Activate your English Pre-intermediate Course book*. © 1996, p. 94: Extract 'Workspace' taken from *English 365 Student's Book 2* by Bob Dignen, Steve Flinders and Simon Sweeney. © 2004, p. 214: illustration from *John Doe* by Antoinette Moses. © 1999. All used by permission of Cambridge University Press; p. 7: illustrations, 'Find the differences' taken from *Collins Cobuild English Course 1* by Jane and Dave Willis. Used by permission of Jane and Dave Willis; p. 27: 'Multiple choices' adapted from *First Certificate Star Student's Book* by Luke Prodromou. © 1998. Reproduced by permission of Macmillan Publishers Ltd; p. 33: 'Britney Spears interview' adapted from article written by Rosanna Greenstreet, *The Guardian*, 26 February 2000. Used by permission of Rosanna Greenstreet; p. 46: Transcripted dialogue between 2 Neighbours characters, Mike and Libby from TV Show, 'Neighbours'. © Freemantle Media; p. 81: Summary of news article from *Coventry Evening Telegraph* 4 October 2000. Used by permission of Coventry Newspapers Limited; p. 81: Summary of news article from *Yorkshire Post* 28 September 2000. Used by permission of Yorkshire Post Newspapers Ltd; p. 87: Extract from the script *French Lieutenant's Woman* by Harold Pinter. © 1982. Used by permission of Faber and Faber Ltd; p. 90: Dialogue from an episode of Bob the Builder, 'Wendy's Busy Day'. Bob the Builder © 2007 HIT Entertainment Limited and Keith Chapman. All rights reserved. The Bob the Builder name and character, related characters and the Bob figure and riveted logos are trademarks of HIT Entertainment Limited. Reg US. Pat & Tm Off. And in the UK and other countries; p. 106: Script from *After Liverpool* by James Saunders. © 1973, James Saunders. All rights whatsoever in this play are strictly reserved and application for performance etc, must be made before rehearsal to Casarotto Ramsay and Associates Ltd, National House, 60-66 Wardour Street, London W1V 4ND. No performance may be given unless a licence has been obtained; p. 116: dialogue from *The Complete Fawlty Towers* written by John Cleese and Connie Booth. Used by permission of David Wilkinson Associates; p. 150: adapted lyrics 'Father and Son' words and music by Cat Stevens © Copyright 1970 Cat Music Limited. Sony Music Publishing (UK) Limited. All Rights Reserved. International Copyright Secured; p. 151: adapted lyrics 'Famous Blue Raincoat' words and music by Leonard Cohen. © Copyright 1971 Stranger Music Incorporated, USA. Chrysalis Songs Limited. Used by permission of Music Sales Limited. All Rights Reserved. International Copyright Secured; p. 154: Script from *Monty Python's Flying Circus Vol 2*. Used by permission Python (Monty) Pictures Ltd; pp. 222-223: Script from the film *Mulholland Drive* by David Lynch. Used by kind permission of David Lynch; pp. 237-238: script 'Dating Agency' from *Little Britain's Complete Scripts and Stuff, series 2* written by Matt Lucas and David Walliams. © Copyright 2005. Used by permission of Matt Lucas and David Walliams.

Photos

p. 33 Britney Spears photo by Vince Bucci © Vince Bucci/Getty Images.

Introduction

Hi. Welcome to this book. How are you doing? Do you want a cup of tea while you're reading?

This is rather an odd way to start a book, especially one which aims to look at the way in which dialogues can be used in language teaching and learning. Of course I cannot really offer you a cup of tea, and I can't even be sure that you drink tea! There may also be issues of register: I have adopted quite an informal style in what I have said to you, and I have no way of telling whether this is appropriate. On the other hand, there is a sense in which entering into dialogue with the people who are going to read this book is a good idea.

I'm assuming that, if you are reading this, then you are somehow involved in the teaching of languages. You are probably a busy teacher and are looking for some practical activities that you can do with your students. You may even be thinking about skipping this introduction and going straight to the sections with the activities. At the same time, you may be wondering about what exactly I mean by dialogue, and whether this book will offer you anything in the way of new ideas.

By anticipating the questions that you may be asking, I am engaging you in a kind of dialogue. It is a bit one-sided, in that I am only imagining what you might want to ask, but of course, if I've got this totally wrong, you will probably have stopped reading already!

All genuine language use, either spoken or written, is essentially dialogic. It exists because of a need to communicate an idea or a feeling to somebody else, and in response to some previous communication – either actual or assumed. As the Russian linguist Mikhail Bakhtin observed, 'Any utterance – the finished, written utterance not excepted – makes response to something that is calculated to be responded to in turn. *It is but one link in a continuous chain of speech performances.*'[1]

1 As quoted in Michael Holquist, *Dialogism: Bakhtin and His World*, London, Routledge, 1991, p. 59.

Writers need to communicate with readers who they may have never met – and in a way which will have general relevance. Speakers, on the other hand, because they tend to have their listener in front of them, are able to talk in a way that they can modify exactly to suit the person who is listening. It is this form of spoken dialogue, exemplified by the first line, that this book is principally concerned with.

What exactly do we mean by dialogue?

Dictionaries define dialogue in three main ways:

1 the lines used by characters in drama or fiction
2 a conversation between two or more people
3 a process of negotiation through speech.

All of these definitions are relevant to the approach to dialogue taken here. Throughout the chapters, there are activities which focus on asking learners to understand, analyse, reproduce, reconstruct, memorise, rehearse, perform, create and communicate lines of dialogue. There are also activities which encourage learners to engage in natural conversation and to negotiate their intended meanings. However, for the purposes of this book, I would like to be more specific about how exactly a dialogue activity may be defined.

- Dialogue is (usually) spoken interaction between (typically) two people, and/or the record of that interaction.
- It may be *pre-scripted* (as in the case of many coursebook dialogues for example, or of play scripts etc.) or it may be *unscripted* (as in the case of improvised dialogues and chat etc.
- It may be *real* (as in naturally occurring talk) or *simulated* (as in the case of film scripts etc. or of classroom dialogues, written to display some particular language point).
- It can be recorded, either as audio or video, or written – or both.
- It may be coursebook-authored, teacher-authored, student-authored or other-authored.
- It may be *form-focused* – i.e. designed to display some feature of grammar or lexis, or some functional exponent; or *meaning-focused*, i.e. intended as a vehicle for information exchange, or both.
- It can be *transactional* – as when someone is asking for information or buying groceries; or it can be *interactional* – as when two friends meet and chat about the weather.

- It may take the form of student–student or student–teacher or student–other (e.g. a guest to the class).

A brief history of dialogue in language learning

Dialogues as a model for real-life interaction

Towards the end of the sixteenth century, an influx of refugees into Britain meant that there was a sudden need for English teachers and teaching materials which could help to equip these people with the ability to communicate effectively in English. One successful teacher and writer of this time was Jacques Bellot, whose book *Familiar Dialogues*, published in 1586, consisted almost entirely of dialogues of everyday conversations, together with a French translation and a pronunciation guide. It is clear, from the following example, that Bellot wrote the dialogues to include examples of situational language that his students would need in their day-to-day lives.

The Poulterer:	What doe you buye?
Ralf:	Showe me a coupell of good, and fatte Rabettes.
The Poulterer:	Here be them, that be very good and fat.
Ralf:	They be very stale.
The Poulterer:	Truely, they be very new.
Ralf:	How sell you them? How much?
The Poulterer:	Ten pence the couple.
Ralf:	It is to much, you are to, deare. They be not worth so much. They be worth but a grote.
The Poulterer:	They be not mine for that price. They coast me more.

Interestingly, the idea of providing learners with short dialogues as models for real-life interaction was also adopted almost four centuries later by A. S. Hornby and others, as the backbone of *the situational approach*. Dialogues like the one below (from *Situational Dialogues* by Michael Ockenden, 1972, p. 48) were intended to be practised and eventually memorised, in order to equip students with the language they needed to function in the host community. Though the language used is significantly closer to the varieties of English used in Britain today, the content of the dialogue is similarly tied to the time at which it was written.

Asking for change

A: Excuse me, but could I trouble you for some change?
B: Let me see. Do you want coppers or silver?

A: I want to make a trunk call.
B: You'd better have silver, then.

Dialogues as a source of language input

As well as serving as models of day-to-day talk, dialogues were also being used as contexts in which to present grammar and functional expressions. In the *audiolingual approach* of the 1950s and 1960s, based on the principles of *behaviourism*, language mastery was seen as the acquisition of good language habits. Central to this approach was the use of specially written dialogues, incorporating the repeated use of a particular structure. This structural approach survived into the 1970s and beyond, and was developed into an 'art form' in the *Streamline* series (Bernard Hartley and Peter Viney, 1978). The example below is from the elementary book *Departures* (the first coursebook I ever used!). Despite being set in a hairdresser's, this dialogue is not transactional, and may have less immediate usefulness to learners as a model for a real-life situation than Bellot's or Ockenden's dialogues. Moreover, since it was contrived in order to display pre-selected grammatical features, it has a rather artificial style. It does, however, provide a humorous and therefore memorable context in which learners can focus on the form and use of *can* to express ability. It also demonstrates a range of vocabulary items which can be used with the structure (*speak French*, *play football*, *sew* etc.).

At the hairdresser's

Jane: . . . Oh yes, my husband's wonderful!
Sally: Really? Is he?
Jane: Yes, he's big, strong and handsome!
Sally: Well, my husband isn't very big, or strong . . . but he's very intelligent.
Jane: Intelligent?
Sally: Yes, he can speak six languages.
Jane: Can he? Which languages can he speak?
Sally: He can speak French, Spanish, Italian, German, Arabic and Japanese.
Jane: Oh! . . . My husband's very athletic.
Sally: Athletic?
Jane: Yes, he can swim, ski, play football, cricket and rugby . . .
Sally: Can he cook?
Jane: Pardon?
Sally: Can your husband cook? My husband can't play sports . . . but he's an excellent cook.

Jane: Is he?
Sally: Yes, and he can sew, and iron . . . he's a very good husband.
Jane: Really? Is he English?

With the development of a more communicative approach to language teaching, such contrived dialogues fell out of favour. Authenticity became the standard by which language data was judged. Moreover, improved recording and transcribing techniques meant that naturally occurring spoken language could be captured and used for teaching purposes. Carter and McCarthy's *Exploring Spoken English* (1997), for example, consists of transcripts of naturally occurring conversations between native speakers. Reading the scripts, listening to the recordings and working through the notes that follow, help to raise awareness about the typical features of spoken language.

The short extract below (also called *At the hairdresser's*) displays a variety of these features, such as hesitation devices (*ermm* – line 13), binominals (*nice and short* – line 14), discourse markers (*you know* – lines 15 and 24, *like* – line 23 and *so, right, yeah* – line 26), backchannels (*yeah* – line 17), ellipsis (*so whispy there* – line 20), heads (*this back bit do you tend to have that bit clippered?* – line 22), false starts (. . . *I have, I tend to have* . . . – line 23), informal language (*cos* – line 27) and vague language (*kind of* – line 24 and *side-ish* – line 28).

At the hairdresser's

12 (S 01)[2] How much do you want off?
13 (S 02) Ermm [2 secs] Well I like to keep the top quite long [(S 01)
14 yeah] ermm, but I like the back nice and short and the sides
15 nice and short. It's just got a bit, you know, a bit grown out of
shape
Too heavy
16 (S 01)
17 (S 02) Yeah.
18 (S 01) Do you have your sides feathered?
19 (S 02) Yeah, yeah.
20 (S 01) So whispy there
21 (S 02) Yeah.
22 (S 01) Now, this back bit do you tend to have that bit clippered?
23 (S 02) Yeah, and I have, I tend to have it like graduated at the back,
right at

[2] 'S' stands for 'Speaker'.

24 the bottom really short and then kind of graduated up, you know
25 not like a line as such, just [(S 01) Right] graded up
26 (S 01) So, right yeah.
27 (S 02) And I generally style it, but it's cos it's got so, I generally have like a
28 maybe side, side-ish parting

Dialogue as language practice

Dialogues have always been used both as sources of input and as a way of structuring language practice (i.e. output). Under audiolingualism this practice function was tightly controlled. The basic procedure for dialogue practice was as follows:

1 Students listen to a dialogue containing key structures to be focused on.
2 They repeat each line of the dialogue after the recording.
3 Certain key words or phrases in the dialogue are changed, and it is practised by the class.
4 A range of choral and individual drills are used to practise forming the key structures.

Again, the advent of the communicative approach and the decline of both situational language teaching and audiolingualism heralded an emphasis on using language for real purposes. Activities which promoted fluency (as opposed to purely accuracy) were prioritised, and memorisation and practice of dialogues consequently became less fashionable.

Dialogue now took on a new role in the classroom. As it involves both a message communicator and a message recipient, dialogue provided the natural format in which communicative language use could occur. Communicative activities involving some kind of 'information gap' became very popular. In an information gap activity, information is distributed among students who, in order to complete a task, are compelled to communicate to share this information. 'Spot the differences' is a typical (and still popular) example of such a task. It involves the students working in pairs. Each student is given a picture which they do not show to their partner. The pictures are slightly different from each other, and the students' task is to find out what the differences are, by asking each other questions ('Is the first person wearing a hat?', 'Has she got long hair?' etc.). The example on the facing page is from *The Collins Cobuild English Course* by Jane and Dave Willis (1988).

PAUL SMITH & SONS
ESTATE AGENTS
214 High Street
FOR SALE
TO LET
OPEN
OPEN
CLOSED ON
WEDNESDAYS

PAUL SMITH & SON
ESTATE AGENTS
215 High Street
Tel: 63390
FOR SALE
TO LET
OPEN
OPEN
ALL
DAY
SUNDAY

Another, more creative and less controlled, dialogue-based activity which gained in favour with the communicative approach, was the use of simulation and roleplay. This was popular because it provided opportunities for students to use language creatively and spontaneously in situations that mirrored real-life ones. At the same time they were 'safe' environments in which students could take risks, since the learners were not genuinely responsible for the effect of their utterances.

Students may be told what their role is, or given a role card (see the example below from *Eight Simulations* by Ken Jones, 1983). After some planning time, perhaps in consultation with other students who have been given the same role, the students engage in dialogue with other learners who have other roles. Again the emphasis is on dialogue as a means to achieving something (in this case, agreement over whether or not a bridge should be constructed) rather than practising specific language items for the sake of it.

Burns – contractor

You are the managing director of Collins and Sons, the civil engineering contractors. You believe the design of the bridge is superb and that the price is realistic. You have spent a lot of money doing research and preparing plans, so it is important that the bridge is built to repay this expenditure.

There has been a lot of opposition to the scheme in the press.

Persuade the members of the public to support the plan.

Dialogue as the medium of instruction

So far we have been looking at the role of dialogue as part of the *content* of language instruction. But dialogue can also be viewed as the *process* of language instruction. According to this view, all learning is dialogic. That is, learning is jointly constructed through the interaction between the learner and a 'better other' (whether parent, sibling, peer, teacher or supervisor). This process of joint construction is conducted largely or entirely through dialogue, and has occurred throughout the history of human interaction.

In Bjorn Kurten's fictional but very probable account of the meeting between Neanderthals and Homo sapiens about 35,000 years ago (*Dance of the Tiger: A Novel of the Ice Age*), Tiger, the young Homo sapien hero, is injured and taken to a Neanderthal settlement, where he is gradually nursed to full recovery. It is through dialogue, rather than any form of formal instruction, that Tiger starts to learn the language of his hosts. Initially he listens to, and begins to understand, the dialogue occurring around him, and then later manages to enter into dialogue himself with the native speakers who have been looking after him. A turning point in his language development is when, after hearing the phrase many times by those around him, he is able to look at one of the people nursing him and say, 'see you tomorrow' in the Neanderthal language.

The idea that language learning can happen through interaction between more proficient and less proficient speakers was used extensively by proponents of the *direct method*. This was developed towards the end of the nineteenth century as a reaction to the more cerebral *grammar–translation approach*. With a strict ban on either the teacher or students using the mother tongue of the learners, teacher to student question and answer sessions were used extensively and were often set up in such a way as to challenge the learners to use language items from the questions in the answers they gave. One early practitioner of the method (a teacher of French) described a typical direct method lesson in these terms: 'It is a conversation during two hours *in the French language* with twenty persons who know nothing of this language. After five minutes only, I am carrying on a dialogue with them, and this dialogue does not cease.'[3]

More recently, there has been increased interest in what is called a *dialogic pedagogy*. This has been influenced by the writings of, among others, Lev Vygotsky (a Russian cognitive psychologist) and Paulo Freire (a Brazilian educationalist). In what is now commonly called 'sociocultural learning theory', Vygotsky emphasised the idea that knowledge is socially constructed through dialogue with more capable speakers. Freire's approach to teaching literacy in Brazil rejected the idea of learning being the transmission of a body of knowledge from teacher to learner, and stressed instead the idea that the content of learning will come out of a process of dialogue between both parties.

The following extract illustrates the way that dialogue can help co-construct learning. It comes from a chat I had with a native speaker of Chilean Spanish on the Santiago metro. The dialogue provided a safe framework (or *scaffold*) in which I could experiment with the Spanish word for 'crawl'.

[3] *Causeries avec mes élèves* (*Conversations with My Students*), Sauveur, 1874.

Me:	Y cuantos meses tiene el tuyo? (and how many months old is yours?)
Hombre:	Nueve (nine)
Me:	Y gatilla? (and does he 'pull the trigger?')
Hombre:	Gatea? Gatea. Si (crawl? He crawls. Yeah.)

Despite pronouncing the word incorrectly, the other speaker understood what I'd meant, reformulated the inaccuracy, and continued with the conversation. As a result of this short exchange, I was moved much closer to being able to use the Spanish verb *gatear* more appropriately the next time I needed to, in an unsupported environment.

Another important aspect of the above exchange, and where it differs significantly from strategies employed by direct method teachers, is that the question is initiated by the learner rather than by the teacher, and is motivated by the need to have a genuine question answered.

In the language classroom, 'scaffolded learning opportunities' can occur between student and teacher, or indeed between the students themselves. They may take place, in fact, in any situation where there is a difference in level, however minimal, between speakers. Some advocates of dialogic pedagogy would argue, however, that, in classrooms heavily influenced by the communicative approach, where there is an emphasis on extensive student-to-student dialogue, the importance of *student-to-teacher* dialogue has sometimes been overlooked.

Who is this book for?

This book is for anyone involved in the teaching of languages and the training of language teachers. New teachers and experienced teachers alike will find a wealth of activities that can be used with their students, many requiring little in the way of preparation and materials, which aim to improve students' speaking and listening skills through challenging them to process or enhance the language content of dialogues.

In many ways this book is an exemplification and a celebration of the ways in which dialogue and dialogues have been previously used in language education. Throughout the chapters, there are dialogue activities which have their roots in everything from situational language teaching through to dialogic pedagogy. At the same time I hope that there are activities which explore dialogues in new ways, and which teachers will be able to adapt to their own teaching contexts and make their own.

How are the activities organised?

There is a gradual progression throughout this book from activities which ask the learners to access dialogues receptively (i.e. through listening to them and reading them) through to those which focus on learner production and creation of dialogues.

'Understanding' and 'Analysing' (Chapter 1 and Chapter 2) challenge the learners to process spoken or written dialogues for either content and meaning or linguistic form.

In 'Reproducing and reconstructing' (Chapter 3) this processing becomes more demanding, as learners are asked to negotiate and make decisions about how language in dialogues hangs together.

'Memorising' (Chapter 4) and 'Rehearsing and performing' (Chapter 5) use dialogues as language practice, requiring the learners to work with dialogues which have already been created.

Then in 'Co-constructing' (Chapter 6) and 'Creating and personalising' (Chapter 7) the onus is on the learners to plan and create dialogues, with ever decreasing teacher support and ever increasing freedom to experiment.

'Communicating' (Chapter 8) and 'Dialogue as learning' (Chapter 9) explore more spontaneous dialogue production, and view dialogue as a means to exchanging ideas and information, and as a way of promoting learning itself.

Dialogues for receptive use

The first half of this book focuses mainly on the use of dialogues as a source of information and ideas, a model of language and a springboard for discussion. Whilst the dialogues themselves are used passively (i.e. the learners are not expected to immediately incorporate their content into natural speech) most of the activities are designed in such a way as to encourage real talk around their content.

Choosing and designing dialogues

There are a number of factors to be considered when choosing a dialogue to be used with a class, or indeed, when designing your own.

Purpose

The purpose for which the dialogue is to be used is an important factor in determining its choice and design. Is the purpose of using the dialogue to provide the learners with practice in understanding spoken language, for example? Or is it to illustrate to the learners how particular language items work in context? Is it to provide a model of a complete stretch of discourse? Does it serve as a springboard for discussion or other activities?

Naturalness

There are advantages in using dialogues which replicate those that the learners may encounter in the world outside the classroom. Apart from anything else, such dialogues are good preparation for real-life language use. And if students begin to notice linguistic features of dialogues used in class, and they can see a link between these and the ones they hear or read outside, then there is a good chance that we are helping to equip them with the skills to start doing this on their own.

At the same time, there will also be a lot of authentic dialogues which are less suitable for classroom use because they contain language which is relatively infrequent, or which, for other reasons, is inappropriate for the needs of the learners. Care should be taken that intelligibility and usefulness are not sacrificed in the name of authenticity. Because of its idiomaticity and speed, much authentic language use is simply beyond the processing skills of any but the most advanced learners.

Familiarity

The more 'known' language that a dialogue contains, the easier it will be for the learners to understand it. (Of course 'knowing' all of the individual words in a dialogue is not the same as 'knowing' how each one works with others to form grammatical structures and chunks of formulaic language.) If the learners are expected to reconstruct, memorise, rehearse or perform the dialogue in some way, then it is reasonable to expect that a high proportion of the language items should be ones that they are already familiar with. The difference in level between their own use of English and that used in the dialogue should not be so great as to make the learning of new language items an impossible task.

If, on the other hand, the dialogue is being used, not for production, but mainly to develop reading or listening skills (Chapter 1), or to raise awareness about the linguistic features it contains (Chapter 2), then the percentage of 'unknown' language items can be greater. In fact, if a dialogue used for this latter purpose does not incorporate linguistic features which are beyond the language level of the students, there may be little point in using it.

Practicability

Dialogues containing very long turns, where only one speaker is speaking, are clearly less useful in terms of highlighting features of dialogic interaction, such as backchannelling, speech acts and adjacency pairs (see Chapter 2), than those with shorter turns.

The overall length of a dialogue is also a factor. It is important that there is sufficient material to provide clues about context, and to display a range of other features. However, learners will be less motivated to work with dialogues which are overlong, especially if they are asked to reproduce them in some way. In many cases dialogues of fewer than ten lines will provide a sufficient quantity of material to work with.

Dialogues for productive use

The second half of this book focuses principally on the use of dialogue as a way of promoting interactive talk. This does not mean that the learners are simply left to talk without any opportunities for reflection or a focus on form. Dialogue activities aim to encourage speaking but they also aim to encourage *thinking about speaking*.

Planning time

Incorporating a planning stage before the learners engage in dialogue can help to build a bridge between the learners' passive knowledge and their capacity to use this knowledge in spontaneous speech. Learners often encounter difficulties when trying to naturally incorporate recently learnt language items into meaning-focused exchanges. By asking them to write a dialogue using a particular set of language items, we effectively 'slow down' the process of speech and create opportunities for more reflective language use. If learners are asked to construct a dialogue in pairs or small groups before they perform it, there is the opportunity for peer teaching of language to occur. Also, producing a written version of the dialogue activates both the written and spoken form of the language included.

On the other hand, there will also be advantages in sometimes encouraging learners to enter into dialogue spontaneously, without asking them to plan the content at all. This, after all, reflects the circumstances in which the learners' real-life dialogue use will occur. Providing the learners with practice in spontaneous interaction in the classroom should help to equip them with the skills they need to interact in such a way in the real world.

Talking time

In this book, productive dialogues fall into two basic categories: those that have been pre-scripted, and those that have not.

With pre-scripted dialogues, the learners are not really communicating anything new, so they cannot be expected to keep mindlessly repeating the same dialogue in the same way. Varying the tasks which the learners are expected to do with the dialogue can help to maintain interest and motivation. For instance learners can be asked to:

- *change the audience* (perform the dialogue to different pairs or groups)
- *change the style* (perform their dialogue so that it is whispered or shouted, or as if they are very tired, or very old etc.)
- *change the context (*perform the dialogue whilst walking down the street, eating breakfast or passing a ball to each other etc.)
- *increase the challenge* (try to perform the dialogue without looking at the text, or very quickly, or without looking at each other etc.)
- *modify the contents* (perform the dialogue with one or two changes in the lines)
- *expand out* (perform the dialogue to include a few lines that came before or after it).

In the case of more spontaneous dialogues, a motivating topic for discussion should ensure that the students are actively engaged. Students are far more likely to want to enter into dialogue if there is a genuine purpose to the interaction and they are not simply talking for the sake of it.

There may be occasions, in monolingual classes, where students break into the mother tongue during dialogue activities. This may be indicative that the task is too challenging for their current level and a simpler task can be given. Or it may show that the importance of trying to perform dialogue tasks in English needs to be discussed with the whole group. Using the mother tongue of the class, if necessary, you can emphasise the usefulness of the effort involved in finding the words in English (as long as it is not too frustrating).

As with pre-scripted dialogues, regular swapping of partners will also be useful with more spontaneous dialogues. (See the next section for some ideas as to how to do this.) Engaging in a similar dialogue on a number of occasions with different people can enhance performance and confidence, and vocabulary range and overall accuracy may increase each time. This repetition of dialogues may occur during one lesson or as a thread which occurs over a number of classes. Of course, repeating a dialogue too many times will have a negative effect on how motivating it is, and the process works best when it is interspersed with brief periods of planning or reflection.

Reflection time

Instead of asking learners to think about the language content of dialogues before engaging with them, another approach is to encourage reflection afterwards. Sometimes having a dialogue with someone is a useful way of raising awareness about the need for input in certain areas of language, and of making the learner more open to to this input. For the teacher it is also an opportunity to observe issues of pronunciation, vocabulary range and accuracy etc.

One way of encouraging reflection is to ask the students to comment in pairs or small groups on what was said or how it was expressed. How successful did they feel they were in communicating what they intended to, and/or in speaking accurately? This can help to reinforce the forms of language items which, up to that point, may have been processed only for their meaning.

Another way is for the teacher to monitor dialogues carefully and make a note of interesting, effective or incorrect language use by students. These can be written up on the board exactly as they were said or in reformulated versions. The students are then asked to analyse or correct each utterance, or to remember who they think each one was said by.

Setting up and managing dialogue

Dialogue is interaction between two people, so obviously pairwork is the best format for practising it in class. Pairwork also allows all the class to be engaged at the same time. Many of the activities in this book will involve the students working in pairs. This applies as much to earlier chapters, where the learners are asked to reflect on and analyse dialogues, as it does to later ones, where the focus is more on reproducing or creating them. Students for whom working in pairs is a new idea may need initial encouragement and/or an explanation (in the learner's first language if necessary) as to why this approach may be useful. It can also be helpful to demonstrate the pairwork activity yourself with another learner to provide a model of how the dialogue can take shape. There are of course a range of formats that pairwork in the classroom can take.

Closed pairs

After making it clear what is going to be discussed, and with a clear signal from the teacher, the students in the class all turn to the person on their left or their right and start talking. The teacher is able to monitor by moving around the different pairs, but in a large class it will be difficult to hear everybody's dialogue.

Open pairs

In this form two students engage in dialogue whilst the rest of the class listens. This can serve as a model for the closed pairwork which is to follow. Or it can provide an opportunity for individual pairs to 'perform' (more accurately or more fluently) what they have been 'rehearsing' in closed pairs.

Back-to-back pairs

This can be used for telephone dialogues or other situations where you want to omit visual clues and encourage the learners to communicate through the sound of their words alone. A slightly less challenging and quieter variation is side-by-side pairs, where learners sit next to each other but try not to look at each other whilst they are talking.

Line dance formation

Students stand in two rows, facing one another, and enact their dialogue. At a given signal from the teacher, the student at the head of one row moves to the tail of that same row and all the other students in that row move up one, so that they have a new partner. They then re-enact their dialogue with their new partner.

Dyadic circles

The students stand in two circles, one inside the other, the students in the inner circle facing those in the outer. There should be an equal number of people in each circle. The students start a dialogue with the person facing them. At a given signal from the teacher the outer circle moves round one place so that everyone is now facing a different person. They now start a new dialogue on a similar or different topic. This can be repeated many times. If the class is small, the students can be seated in two concentric circles of chairs.

Milling

The whole class stand up in a space where they are free to move around. They engage in dialogue with a person of their choosing and then move on to somebody new when the dialogue has reached a natural conclusion, or at a given signal from the teacher. This type of pairwork is particularly suited to conducting various forms of survey.

The ever widening gap

The students stand in two lines facing each other in the middle of the room. They start talking to the person who is opposite them. As they continue their conversation they move gradually away from each other by walking slowly backwards. Eventually the students are at opposite ends of the room and have to raise their voices considerably. This is good for students who need to develop the ability to speak more loudly and clearly. The activity can be extended by asking students to move freely around in the space, whilst still continuing to talk to each other.

1 Understanding

An ability to understand the dialogues which students hear and read in the world around them must be a starting point for any dialogue work. The activities in this first chapter all use a written, spoken or written and spoken dialogue as a source of input for the students to engage with.

A traditional approach to developing listening skills in the classroom is to set students a range of tasks to complete whilst listening to the recording of a dialogue. Understanding dialogues: a basic procedure (1.1) and Board grab(1.2) illustrate some of these techniques.

Many learners, however, are also keen to have access to the written form of the dialogue at some point, because it allows processing of the text in a different way. Reading versus listening (1.3) aims to raise students' awareness about the advantages and disadvantages of being able to see the tapescript which often accompanies spoken coursebook dialogues.

Dialogue interpretation worksheets (1.4), Jigsaw (1.5), and Designing exam questions (1.6) turn things on their head, and use the written form of the dialogue as the point of entry for the learners. The students first read the dialogue, then they listen to it. This requires a different kind of processing.

In What are they talking about? (1.7), Snippets (1.8) and Fairy tale tableaux (1.9) the learners are exposed to only the written format of quite short dialogues and encouraged to interpret the wider context in which the dialogue occurs.

Lame jokes (1.10) and Working with interviews (1.11) check students' understanding of dialogues by asking them to match questions with answers, and finally in Dialogue as a way into a graded reader (1.12) and The bit I like (1.13), understanding a dialogue is the springboard for more extensive reading work.

1.1 Understanding dialogues: a basic procedure

Outline	Students listen to a dialogue and work through a series of tasks aimed at helping them understand the dialogue
Focus	Checking understanding of a spoken dialogue
Level	Elementary plus
Time	20 minutes plus

Materials and preparation Choose a spoken dialogue appropriate to the level and interests of your group. Design a series of tasks to go with it. The example below is the transcript of a telephone dialogue between someone enquiring about train times and prices, and a voice-activated information service.

Procedure

1. Tell the class what the topic of the dialogue is (in this case asking for information over the phone). Ask the students for their views. Is this common in their country/countries? What kinds of information can be accessed in this way? Do they prefer getting information like this or do they prefer talking with somebody face to face? Which is easier? How do they feel about doing it in English? Why? These questions can be discussed in small groups or with the whole class together.
2. Set a task to focus on overall understanding of the conversation. This can often be captured by asking four wh-questions: who is talking to whom, about what, where and why? (In the example below a customer is talking to a voice-activated service over the phone, in order to gain information about train times and prices.)
3. Play the recording and ask the class to compare and discuss their answers in pairs.
4. Conduct feedback with everybody together.
5. Now set a task to focus on more detailed understanding. For instance the learners could be given the following statements and asked to decide, while listening, whether they are true or false.

   The passenger wants to travel to Liverpool.
   The journey takes more than two hours.
   The passenger is travelling alone.
   The passenger wants to come back by train on the same day.
   The passenger wants to know how much the ticket will be.

6. Play the recording again. The learners compare and discuss their answers and feedback is conducted as before.
7. Set up a situation where students have to engage with a similar topic to the one they have listened to. For instance the learners could take part in a roleplay situation, where one person asks for information about trains, and the other provides it.

Box 1

A: Welcome to Virgin Trains. If you're new to this voice-activated service just say 'Help'. Here are your options. You can plan a journey, buy tickets or enquire about an existing booking. Which would you like to do?
B: Plan a journey.
A: Would you like to get fare information or just check the timetable?
B: Check the timetable.
A: OK. What train journey would you like to hear timetable information for? An example is London to Manchester.
B: Birmingham New Street to Liverpool.
A: Thanks. And what date would you like to travel?
B: Tomorrow.
A: And what time? For example 12 midday or arriving by 4 in the afternoon. If you like you can say 'first train' or 'last train'. So what time?
B: Arriving by 2 in the afternoon.
A: So you want Birmingham New Street to Liverpool on Sunday 16th April, arriving by 2 in the afternoon. Did I get that right?
B: Yes.
A: OK I'll check the timetable. PAUSE. Thanks for holding. I'm still checking the timetable. PAUSE. Here you go. There's a train leaving Birmingham New Street at 11:30 in the morning and gets into Liverpool Lime Street at 1:08 in the afternoon. I can check other times if you say 'earlier trains' or 'later trains'. If the journey's OK say 'continue'. Otherwise you can change any of the journey details by saying 'change details'.
B: Continue.
A: Alright. Do you want a return journey?
B: No.
A: Great. Now that you've planned your journey you can buy tickets, check fares or get further assistance.
B: Check fares.
A: How many adults will be travelling?
B: One.
A: Any children?
B: No.
A: Do you have any railcards?
B: No.
A: Thank you. Please hold while I connect you to an agent.

Variations

a Set up the roleplay activity before doing any of the listening exercises. This is a good way of engaging interest from the start, and raising awareness about the gap between the learners' use of English and that used by more proficient speakers.

b Play the tape without any of the preparatory work. After listening, students discuss with a partner everything that they understood and can remember from the dialogue.

c Give out the dialogue as a jumbled series of lines. Students work in pairs to put the lines of the dialogue in order. They then listen to check whether their order is the same as in the recording.

d After they have listened to the recording for the first time, tell the class that they are going to be asked some more questions about the dialogue. Ask them to listen to it again and try to retain as much information as they can. Now give out the set of detailed understanding questions and ask the learners to discuss the answers in pairs.

e Give out the transcript after students have completed all the listening tasks. Ask them to listen again whilst reading it. This is a useful opportunity to focus on language which may otherwise go unnoticed. For instance, with the dialogue in Box 1, the learners could be asked to read and identify all the features which indicate that this is a voice-activated service, as opposed to a conversation between real people.

f Prepare a copy of the transcript with gaps in it. The missing language items should include areas which it would be useful for the class to focus on. After the other listening task/tasks, give out the gapped version of the transcript and ask the students to decide on a suitable word or phrase to go in each space. They then listen again to check.

1.2 Board grab

Outline	Students run to the board in a race to grab language items that they hear from a dialogue. This activity is suitable for classes of up to 15 students. For larger classes see the variation below
Focus	Developing aural recognition skills, reviewing dialogues and reinforcing previously encountered lexical chunks
Level	Any
Time	5 minutes plus
Materials and preparation	On large pieces of paper, write out a selection of language items from a dialogue which the students have listened to in a previous lesson. These could include formulaic expressions (chunks), discourse

markers, individual words or examples of specific grammar structures. Include some items which are not mentioned in the dialogue. (See the example in Box 2 from *Language in Use: Upper Intermediate*, Recording 4.1 – the last three chunks were not included in the recording.) Stick them up randomly all over the board. Find the relevant part of the recording of the dialogue. Each student will also need access to the complete transcript of the recording.

Procedure

1 Invite the class up to the front and organise the students so that they are standing in a semi circle around the board. Make sure no one is hovering too close to it.
2 Draw the students' attention to the words or phrases on the board. Tell them that some of the items were in the dialogue that they heard in the previous lesson. Ask them to discuss with a partner which ones they think are included.
3 Split the class into two teams by dividing them down the middle. Tell them that if they hear one of the language items, they have to run up to the board, grab the appropriate piece of paper and take it back to their team. The team with the most pieces of paper at the end wins.
4 Play the recording or read out the dialogue and let the race begin.
5 When the recording has finished, count up how many pieces of paper each team has.
6 Give out copies of the complete tapescript (or direct the students to the back of the book) so that they can see how the chunks work in context.

Notes

This activity works well as a warm-up and provokes some very focused scan listening.

I learnt the idea of students grabbing language items from the board from Vicky Wood at International House, Santiago.

Variation for larger classes

Instead of putting the language items up on the board, organise the class into groups of three or four. Give each group a set of the chunks which have been cut up. They then arrange these randomly on the desk in front of them. Each student now tries to grab as many chunks as possible as they listen to the recording.

Box 2

you're about to go
a little bit frightened
looking forward to it
in the first place
it's a good cause
make sure that
supposed to
the second thing is
by heart
it was fantastic
I was kind of forced to
you feel in control
the million dollar question
a bit of a shock
took my breath away
at the last minute

1.3 Reading versus listening

Outline	Students compare and contrast the experience of reading the tapescript versus listening to the recording without it
Focus	Encouraging debate and raising awareness about the advantages and disadvantages of being able to see the tapescript
Level	Pre-intermediate plus
Time	30 minutes plus
Materials and preparation	You will need copies of the tapescript for the listening material you are working with (normally found in the back of the coursebook).

Procedure

1 Do the pre-listening activities suggested in your coursebook with everybody together.

2 Now direct the students' attention to the tasks which go with the listening material, and ask them to try to complete them whilst listening. Give one half of the class the tapescript which accompanies the material.

They can read and listen at the same time. The other half need to complete the tasks through listening alone.

3 Now pair students off so that you have one student who listened with the tapescript working with another who couldn't see it.
4 Encourage them to compare and discuss answers and to discuss whose task they felt was the easiest/most useful and why.
5 Write the following sentence heads on the board and ask the students to complete some of them, so that their opinions are expressed.

It's useful to spend class time reading the tapescript because...

It's more useful to spend class time listening without seeing the tapescript because...

I prefer being able to see the tapescript because...

I prefer just listening without seeing the tapescript because...

6 Invite the students to mingle around and compare and discuss what they wrote.
7 Open things up and have a general debate about the pros and cons of listening with the tapescript versus without it. Broaden the discussion to include the issue of watching English programmes with the dialogue displayed as subtitles at the bottom of the screen.

Possible points:

Looking at the tapescript/subtitles makes it easier to notice the language items that are being used. You can reread bits that you've missed and focus on spelling, contractions, articles etc. more easily. When listening and reading at the same time, you can start to associate the way a word is written with its pronunciation.

However, this isn't really what happens in the world outside the classroom. When people speak to us we don't have the luxury of subtitles! If we always read what is being said we may not be training ourselves to pick up language from hearing it alone.

1.4 Dialogue interpretation worksheets

Outline Students use a worksheet to help them to interpret the contents of a dialogue

Focus Intensive reading skills. Encouraging discussion about ways of interpreting a dialogue and preparing the ground for listening to/watching the recording

Level Intermediate plus

Time 30 minutes plus

Materials and preparation Choose a dialogue from a film, soap opera or comedy sketch which your students will find interesting. You need both the written version and the recording of it. Prepare a worksheet (see the example below in Box 3) which will challenge the students to interpret what is going on. See Dialogue Bank F on p. 237 for an example dialogue for an intermediate group from the comedy series *Little Britain* (Dialogue Bank A on p. 222 could also be used for this activity). Each student will need a copy of the worksheet and the dialogue.

Box 3

Worksheet

1 Read this dialogue to get a general idea of what the people are talking about. Turn to the person next to you and discuss what you remember and how you feel about it.

2 What do you think is the relationship between the characters (Roy, Margaret and Mr Mann)? What helped you to work this out?

3 Below are some adjectives to describe character and feelings. Can you match any of them to any of the characters? Use a dictionary if you need to. You do not necessarily need to use all of the words. What things that the characters say helped you to decide?

strange	*patient*	*rude*	*difficult*
fussy	*annoying*	*annoyed*	*polite*

4 Mr Mann's answers in lines 13, 15, 17 and 19 are quite strange. What would be a more 'normal' answer for each question?

5 How do you think the lines 14, 23, 25, 39 are said? Try saying them with your partner.

6 Do you think you would behave differently if you were Roy?

7 This dialogue was written to make people laugh. At which points in the dialogue do you think the audience will laugh when they hear it?

Procedure

1 Give out copies of the dialogue and the worksheet to the students.

2 Encourage the students to discuss the answers to the questions in pairs. Depending on the group, it may be more appropriate to allow them time to go through the worksheet on their own first, before discussing answers.

3 Bring the class together to discuss some of their interpretations with everyone.
4 Now play the recording of the dialogue and ask the class to compare it with how they saw the written version. Is there anything that they now interpret differently?

1.5 Jigsaw

Outline	After reading the scripts for different scenes, students swap information about what they have read. They then watch the complete section to compare it with how they had imagined it
Focus	Encouraging learners to access and activate information contained in a script
Level	Pre-intermediate plus
Time	30 minutes plus
Materials and preparation	Choose two adjacent scenes including dialogue from a film or soap opera, or divide one scene into two fairly equal parts. You will need copies of the script of both scenes and the DVD that goes with it. See Dialogue Bank A on pp. 222–225 for an example from the film *Mulholland Drive* by David Lynch. (Dialogue Bank F on pp. 237–238 could also be used for this activity.)

Procedure

1 Give one side of the class the script of the first scene and the other side the script of the second one. Ask the students to read it and work out the basic details of where the people are, what they are doing, what happens and what they are talking about. It may help to write these categories on the board.
2 In pairs or small groups, ask the students to discuss what information they have worked out about the scene.
3 Now pair off students so that they are working with somebody who has read the other scene. Ask them to share as much information as they can about what they have read. What do they think the characters in the scene are like? How old are they? What do they look like? What kind of people are they?
4 Listen to the recording or show the complete scene on the DVD.
5 Discuss whether the characters and the scene were similar to how they had imagined them.

1.6 Designing exam questions

Outline	From looking at the tapescript, students design multiple choice questions and then answer each other's questions
Focus	Raising awareness about the format and style of multiple choice listening questions
Level	Intermediate plus
Time	30 minutes plus
Materials and preparation	Rewrite a set of listening comprehension multiple choice questions so that the option parts are left blank (see the example below from a First Certificate Listening, Part 4, set of questions).

Procedure

1 Divide the class into two equal groups. Give one group one half of the set of questions, and the other group the second half. They also need the part of the tapescript which has the answers to their set of questions.

2 The task for each pair of students within the groups is to find the correct answer from the transcript, write it in, and to also come up with and write in two other incorrect answers in the relevant spaces.

3 Pairs now swap sheets with students from the other half of the class.

4 Play the tape and ask the students to answer the questions they have just received as they listen.

5 Now rearrange the class so that pairs who have answered each other's questions are working together. Tell them to check their answers and to give each other feedback on how difficult the questions were and why. Give out the original options that were provided in the coursebook or exam paper, and ask students to compare them with the questions they designed themselves.

Below are the first three questions relating to exercise 2 on page 164 of *First Certificate Star* by Luke Prodromou. The three multiple choice answers have been completed by students and are uncorrected.

1) What percentage of the population play the lottery every week?
   a) 42%
   b) 90%
   c) 58%

2) If you want to win why should you choose a number like 32 33 35 36 37 39?
   a) Those numbers are logical.

b) Those numbers are unlikely to be chosen by anyone else.
c) The only illogical way to approach the lottery is to be logical.

3) Professor Beaton says playing the lottery is
a) much better than saving the money.
b) having dreams which never come true.
c) because even though people work hard, it is difficult to get by.

Notes

Putting themselves into the role of question designer is useful for students in many ways. Apart from the benefits of seeing the tapescript and making connections between the written and spoken word, awareness is also raised about the way in which 'distractor' answers are thrown in to mislead.

1.7 What are they talking about?

Outline	A dialogue is slowly revealed to the class, who try to interpret the situation in which it is happening
Focus	Predicting content from contextual clues
Level	Elementary plus
Time	5 minutes plus
Materials and preparation	Choose a dialogue in which the topic of conversation is not immediately obvious. See the example below (from the CANCODE corpus) for an intermediate class. Prepare a transparency of the dialogue.

Procedure

1 Reveal the first line of the dialogue on the overhead projecter. Ask for suggestions as to who is speaking, where the dialogue is taking place, and what the purpose of the interaction is.

2 Reveal the next line or couple of lines and see if the learners want to reinterpret how they saw the dialogue. Keep revealing lines and asking for their interpretations until they have worked out as much as is possible.

Extension

Ask the students to find their own dialogues for interpretation as homework. These could be from the coursebook they are using, other coursebooks, or film or television scripts (see also The bit I like (1.13)). Make transparency copies of the dialogues they choose and allow each student a few minutes each lesson to present their own dialogues to the rest of the class as outlined above.

Box 4

A: So that's likely to be the best.
B: And what about capacity?
A: Capacity wise . . . the . . . most of these now take an eleven pound load.
B: Mm.
A: Erm and then coming back to Bosch as I say they're well built including the drum. What they tend to do is put more holes in the drum because it's a thicker drum.
B: Yes.
A: They're able to do that without weakening it.
B: So stainless steel's thicker?
A: More solid.
B: Mm.
A: Erm and they also sort of if you look at the back of them some of them are flat. This is actually moulded so it's always pushing the clothes away from the back.
B: Ah yeah.
A: And these paddles sort of lift it up. Now because there's more holes in the drum they're able to get water in quicker.
B: Mhm.
A: . . . and obviously get it out quicker as well and better.
B: Mhm.
A: And that's why you usually find that . . .
B: Do you price match by the way?
A: Oh yes.
B: You do. Yeah.
A: Yes. Oh yes. I mean if you saw that machine anywhere else cheaper then we would.
B: Yes. I thought. I thought you would.
A: We would naturally match the price.

From the CANCODE Corpus of Spoken English

1.8 Snippets

Outline	Students read a selection of snippets of dialogue, identify the context in each case, and then focus on the language that they contain
Focus	Typical items of spoken language relating to particular contexts
Level	Intermediate plus
Time	30 minutes plus

Materials and preparation	Choose a selection of short snippets of authentic dialogue from Dialogue Bank B on pp. 226–229 (all taken from the CANCODE corpus). Cut them up into individual snippets, being careful to remove the information underneath each dialogue about who the speakers are. Spread them out around the walls of the classroom where students can stand up to read them. Prepare a transparency of one of the snippets (see below).

Procedure

1 Organise the students into pairs.

2 Ask them to go around the room, looking at each of the snippets of dialogue. For each one they should write down who they think the speakers are, and what they are talking about.

3 Encourage the students to compare answers with a different pair.

4 Show the transparency version of one of the snippets. Ask the class to identify the linguistic features which helped them to work out what the topic of conversation was. For example in snippet 1 the students may identify language items like *pause*, *stop*, *play*, *rewind*, *fast forward*, *plug that into your TV* etc., to indicate that they are talking about a camcorder. They may also notice the enthusiastic tone of some of A's language (*So you've got naturally . . .*, *So everything is there for you* etc.), which is typical of someone who is trying to sell something.

5 Now ask them to work in different pairs and to go round some of the dialogues again, making a note of key language items for each one. Encourage dictionary use during this stage. Students again share what they have noticed in small groups.

Extension

Students choose one of the snippets and develop it into a longer dialogue.

1.9 Fairy tale tableaux

Outline	Students prepare tableaux (or still images) to represent snippets of dialogue from fairy tales
Focus	Understanding short snippets of dialogue and developing discussion about scenes from fairy tales
Level	Pre-intermediate plus
Time	30 minutes plus
Materials and preparation	Make copies of the fairy tale snippets from Dialogue Bank C on pp. 230–233 picking out the ones which are most suitable for your group.

Procedure

1 Give each pair of students the list of snippets of dialogue from fairy tales.
2 Ask them to discuss which fairy tale they think each one comes from. What is the moment in the story when this little piece of dialogue occurs? If students are working in multicultural pairings and one of them doesn't know one of the stories, the other person can briefly tell it.
3 Go through the answers with everyone. If some students still don't know some of the stories the class can be rearranged so that students who do know the stories can tell the others.
4 In pairs again, students choose some or all of the snippets and plan a tableau (or still image) which represents the moment in time when each of the dialogues occurred.
5 Now put different pairs together. Each pair has to present their tableau to the other one, who need to work out which dialogue it is representing.

Variation

Instead of making a still image, students mime the scene in which the dialogue occurs or prepare a gibberish version of it (see Gibberish scenes (8.3)).

1.10 Lame jokes

Outline	Students try to find punch lines to complete their jokes
Focus	Raising awareness about the double meanings contained in jokes
Level	Intermediate plus
Time	15 minutes plus
Materials and preparation	Make a copy of some or all of the jokes in Dialogue Bank D on pp. 232–233, and cut each joke up so that questions and punch lines are separated.

Procedure

1 Display the punch lines of the jokes on the walls around the room.
2 Students work in pairs. Each pair is given a first line of a joke. Their task is to go round the room and to find the punch line that goes with their question. When they find it they take it back to you.
3 If the question and the punch line match, then the pair is given a new question for which to find the punch line. If they don't match, they can either go back and try again or swap their question for a new one (having first put the unused punch line back on the wall).
4 The pair with the most complete jokes at the end wins.

Extension

Display the complete jokes around the room. Ask the students to go round again in pairs and to identify what the word with the double meaning is in each of the jokes. Students then tell the jokes they can remember to each other. Which one is the best/worst?

Variation 1

Instead of asking students to go round the room, give small groups of students a set of questions and punch lines to match together. They then tell their favourite jokes to members of other groups.

Variation 2

Select enough jokes so that there is one complete joke for each pair of students in the class. Jumble the lines up and give each student either a punch line or a question. Students now go around the class saying their lines to each other and trying to find the person whose line matches theirs. New pairs now sit together. This is a good way of mixing students up at the start of a lesson.

1.11 Working with interviews

Outline	Students read an interview and try to decide which of the answers have been made up
Focus	Encouraging intensive reading
Level	Pre-intermediate plus
Time	20 minutes plus
Materials and preparation	Find an interview from a newspaper or magazine which would be of interest to your learners. See for instance http://www.metro.co.uk/ for a rich source of interviews written in dialogue format. Rewrite the interview, changing two of the answers but keeping the rest the same (see the Britney Spears example below). Each student needs a copy of the article.

Procedure

1 Give out the accompanying picture for the interview only and discuss with the group everything they know about the person.
2 Now distribute your doctored version of the interview. Students have to read it and work out which answers were made up. They discuss this in pairs.
3 Conduct feedback and, before revealing the correct answers, discuss why they thought particular answers were made up.

Britney Spears

© Vince Bucci/Getty Images

Britney Spears, 18, appeared in TV commercials as a child. At 11, she joined Disney's Mickey Mouse Club, and three years later began a pop career. In 1998, she was the first female artist to have a simultaneous Billboard Number 1 single and album with a debut release. In the UK, Baby One More Time was the fastest selling debut single in history. Spears was recently named best rock or pop newcomer at the US Music Awards.

Compiled by Rosanna Greenstreet

Saturday February 26, 2000
The Guardian

1 **What is your idea of perfect happiness?**
Finding a true soul-mate.

2 **What is your greatest fear?**
I am terrified of heights. I can't even look out of a second floor window.

3 **Which living person do you most admire?**
My mom, because she's loved me unconditionally.

4 **What is the trait you most deplore in yourself?**
I worry too much.

5 **What do you most dislike about your appearance?**
My fingernails – I bite them terribly.

6 **What is your most unappealing habit?**
Biting my fingernails.

7 **What is your favourite word?**
'Amazing'.

8 **What objects do you always carry with you?**
A prayer book.

9 **What makes you depressed?**
When I hear about bad things happening to children.

10 **What is your favourite journey?**
I believe the journey I'm on now will be my favourite.

11 What is your favourite book?
The Bible.

12 Do you believe in capital punishment?
Yes.

13 Which living person do you most despise?
I try to find good in all people and try not to despise anyone.

14 For what cause would you die?
My beliefs.

15 What is your greatest regret?
None at this moment – thankfully.

16 How do you relax?
I watch videos of old silent movies and drink Champagne.

17 What single thing would improve the quality of your life?
The promise of continued good health.

18 What would your motto be?
Always smile.

19 What keeps you awake at night?
Missing my family.

20 Do you believe in life after death?
Yes.

21 How would you like to be remembered?
As someone whose music touched many lives.

22 What is the most important lesson life has taught you?
Be true to yourself.

The answers for questions 2 and 16 have been changed and should read 'Not being able to find a true soul mate' (Question 2) and 'I light candles, put on a great CD and take a bubble-bath' (Question 16).

Variations

a Give out the questions only and ask the students to write answers in role as the celebrity. Pin these up around the room and encourage them to read each other's to decide which is most like what the celebrity would write.

b Distribute the questions and answers jumbled up and ask the students to match them together.
c Give out the questions only and ask the students to do a roleplay of a television interview with the celebrity before reading.
d Give out the answers only and ask students to predict what the questions were.
e Give out the questions and invite the students to mingle and ask and answer the questions themselves first.
f Students do a roleplay of the interview after reading it to see how many of the celebrity's answers they can remember.
g Ask students to read the article again and find answers which they think are good/surprising/boring/stupid/clever/untrue etc.
h Tell the students to cross out all the questions that they wouldn't want to be asked themselves.
i Use two dialogues of a similar style. Give out some jumbled up answers and ask students to predict which answers belong to which celebrity.

Note

Articles about celebrities in the form of a dialogue between an interviewer and the interviewee have become increasingly common in recent years. As they tend to mirror spoken language more than written, and because they involve the reader by attempting to anticipate their questions, they are often easier for learners to access than standard articles. They can also provide a rich source of models of spoken language.

1.12 Dialogue as a way into a graded reader

Outline	The teacher performs the dialogue from the opening part of a graded reader
Focus	Creating interest in a story and helping with comprehension
Level	Any. (The example below is for a beginners class)
Time	10 minutes plus
Materials and preparation	Rewrite the opening part of the reader as a playscript (see the example below). Each student will need a copy of this dialogue. Prepare some comprehension questions that can be asked to check the students' understanding of the gist of the dialogue.

Procedure

1 Tell the class some basic information about who the characters in the dialogue are.

2 Using the script, perform the dialogue in front of the class, taking on both roles yourself. You will need to deliver it sufficiently clearly and slowly for them to understand whilst keeping it as natural as possible. Using physical action and simple props where appropriate will enhance students' understanding of what is happening. (For the example below, only a newspaper and a chair would be necessary.)

3 Ask the class some comprehension questions to check their understanding of the gist of the dialogue. For the example below these could include: Where is Theresa going?, What is Frank's job?, What does Theresa want?

4 Give out the dialogue to the class and allow them to read it. Reread the dialogue to them, encouraging them to follow the written version.

Box 5

TERESA: I'm leaving now.
Frank looks up from his newspaper
TERESA: I'm leaving now. What are you going to do today? Don't go back to bed!
Why don't you go out and look for a job?
FRANK: But I've got a job. I'm a writer.
TERESA: But you never finish your books. You begin lots of books but you never finish them. You need a real job. We must have more money!
FRANK: Why? Why must we have more money?
TERESA: We need money to buy things. You need new clothes. Look at your old clothes!
FRANK: There's nothing wrong with my clothes. My jeans are a little dirty but I can wash them.
TERESA: You do need new clothes. And I want a nice car. And we need a new television!
Frank closes his eyes
TERESA: Open your eyes! Don't go to sleep. I'm talking to you.
FRANK: Look, I'm not sleeping. I'm thinking. Anyway you don't read my books.
TERESA: I read the first half of *Every Morning*. I liked it.
FRANK: Good.
TERESA: I think I'm going to be late home this evening. There's a lot to do at work.
FRANK: Goodbye. Have a nice day.

From *Help*, by Philip Prowse. Cambridge English Readers Level 1

Notes

Depending on the level of the students, it may be appropriate to get a confident learner to take on one of the roles with you at stage 2.

For many learners the dialogue will be the most comprehensible part of a story to access. Starting with the dialogue will hopefully build their confidence in their ability to understand the story as a whole.

1.13 The bit I like . . .

Outline	Students scan websites devoted to film scripts for their favourite scenes
Focus	Developing extensive reading skills, raising awareness about the language learning potential of film scripts, and providing practice in talking about films in English
Level	Strong intermediate plus
Time	1 hour plus
Materials and preparation	Internet access, either at school or at home, is needed for this activity.

Procedure

1 Tell the students to write down the names of three of their favourite films in English. For the purposes of this exercise, it doesn't matter if they have only seen a dubbed version of the film.

2 Ask the students to mingle and to pair off with someone who has mentioned one of the films that they have themselves. Pair off those who haven't found a partner by the end.

3 Encourage them to discuss key moments of dialogue in the story of the film they have chosen, and to choose the most important or best bit of the film to focus on.

4 Send the students to the computer room, if you have one available, and ask them to try to find the section of the film script that they have chosen to focus on on the internet. Websites like www.simplyscripts.com and www.script-o-rama.com have a very large selection of film scripts available online. Also using a search engine like www.google.co.uk and entering the name of the film and the words 'film script' or 'movie script' may prove worthwhile.

5 Ask them to print off or copy out a very short section of the dialogue around their key moment.

6 Put all the names of the films on the board in no particular order. Pin up

all the screenplay extracts around the classroom on the walls and give each one a number. Ask the students to work in their pairs, reading all the extracts and making a note of which film they think each one belongs to.

7 Check the answers together and see which pair got the most right.
8 Ask the students to prepare a short presentation about what their film is about, why they like it, and why they have chosen this particular extract. At some point during the presentation they may include the part of the tapescript that they've picked by taking on the roles themselves and performing it.

Variation

If students have access to the internet outside the school, finding their favourite extract could also be done on an individual basis and as homework. The beauty of this activity is that it encourages a lot of fairly motivating extensive reading. While checking the availability of some of my favourite films on the internet, I ended up sitting up till three in the morning reading the entire film script of *American Beauty* and *Mulholland Drive*!

2 Analysing

In the previous chapter dialogues were used mainly as a source of information and ideas. Here the focus shifts from an emphasis purely on meaning, to an examination of linguistic form. The activities included here challenge the students to notice aspects about the way messages are communicated in dialogues, rather than simply reacting to what is being communicated.

Tapescripts at the back of coursebooks are a useful resource which are often underexploited in the classroom. After doing the content-focused listening exercises in the coursebook, I have often found that asking the students to read the tapescript can raise awareness about language. Sometimes this can lead to a sudden realisation about what was actually being said and can clear up misunderstandings. In my experience many students appreciate these opportunities for close study of the form of spoken language, and this approach makes up for a general lack of such activities in some coursebooks.

Of course it is also useful for students to engage with more authentic dialogues which were not specially produced for language students. Also included here are activities which ask students to analyse the dialogue in poetry, television programmes and transcripts of authentic conversation.

The first four activities (Tricky words, Closed mouth minimal pairs, Fishermen and Stage directions (2.1–2.4)) aim to raise awareness about pronunciation features, and look at ways in which pronunciation affects meaning.

Authentic versus scripted dialogues (2.5) asks students to identify features which distinguish real talk from dialogues which have been written for classrooms, and the next three activities (Dialogue scan race, Filling in and Speech acts (2.6–2.8)) further explore the workings of some of these features.

Finally, the teacher does the speaking test, Student dialogue reformulation and Backchanneling (2.9–2.11) use classroom dialogues as the material to be analysed.

2.1 Tricky words

Outline Students identify areas of a dialogue which are difficult to pronounce and then listen again, paying particular attention to these areas

Focus Encouraging students to notice the pronunciation features of tapescripts

Level Any

Time 15 minutes

Materials and preparation Each student needs a copy of the tapescript for the listening material you are working with.

Procedure

1. After doing the listening tasks from the coursebook, give out copies of the tapescript or direct the students to the tapescripts section at the back of the book. Ask them to underline words or chunks that they would feel unsure about if they had to pronounce them correctly themselves.
2. Invite students to get up and mingle. Ask them to share what they've underlined with others and see if they can find somebody who can help them with the pronunciation. Take a back seat yourself at this stage.
3. In pairs students have a go at saying their underlined bits to each other. Again, do not get involved here. You want them to be very motivated to listen carefully to the tape at the next stage.
4. Play the tape again and ask students to listen out carefully for the words they picked.
5. If it's not too long, ask them to read the tapescript to each other in pairs and to try to incorporate the correct pronunciation of their tricky words.

2.2 Closed mouth minimal pairs

Outline The class take part in a minimal pairs exercise where they are not able to open their mouths. (See also Mimed dialogues (3.13) and Gibberish scenes (8.3))

Focus Raising awareness about the pauses and stress and intonation patterns of utterances in dialogue

Level Any

Time 10 minutes plus

Materials and preparation Pick out some lines from a coursebook dialogue that you've worked with, where there are interesting issues of intonation and stress. Prepare a copy of these lines for each student. Each number on the worksheet should consist of two utterances of similar length. See Box 6 for some examples which are taken (in no particular order) from *Wavelength Elementary*, Recording 100. You will also need the recording that goes with the tapescript.

Procedure

1 After doing the coursebook tasks associated with the recording, put two very different utterances up on the board (e.g. *I feel really tired. I'm going to bed* and *You look really beautiful today*). Say both utterances to the group but keep your mouth firmly closed whilst doing it. Since the individual sounds of both utterances will all now be very similar, the differences between them will be shown by stressed syllables, pauses and the way in which your voice rises or falls. Ask the students to try to work out which utterance is which. Discuss how it was that they were able to work it out.
2 Play the recording again, asking the students to pay particular attention to how the utterances you've picked out are said.
3 Give out the worksheet with the sentences you have chosen. Ask them to experiment with closed mouth versions of the lines. Encourage them to say one of the options for each line and to see if their partner can guess which one it is.
4 Ask pairs to do their favourite ones for the whole group to guess.
5 With students working in pairs again, ask them to practise saying the lines normally now, but trying to incorporate the features they noticed when they did them with mouths closed.

Box 6

1 a He's off sick. He had a very bad week last week.
b Well, for a start, his girlfriend left him.
2 a Oh, you're joking! I thought they were serious.
b Yeah, oh, he was really depressed about it.
3 a Then his brother crashed his car.
b You mean his new sports car?
4 a He was really, really angry.
b He didn't even come to the pub.

Variation

With a multilingual group where students do not know each other's mother tongue, instead of keeping their mouths closed, learners can be asked to say the utterances in their first language. Students need to be paired with someone whose language is significantly different from their own. This is a powerful and fun way of raising awareness about differences between their mother tongues.

2.3 Fishermen

Outline	Students analyse the pronunciation features of a poem
Focus	Raising awareness about linking and weak forms in connected speech
Level	Intermediate plus
Time	30 minutes plus
Materials and preparation	Prepare photocopies of both the original 'Fishermen' poem and the 'translated' version (see Boxes 7 and 8 below).

Procedure

1 Give out copies of the translated version of the poem (Box 7), and establish the details of who the two people are, where they are and what is going on.

2 Ask the students to try out the poem in pairs, with each student taking one of the roles.

3 Discuss with the class how in natural speech certain syllables are stressed much more than others and some might even disappear completely. Exemplify this by writing *What do you want?* on the board and asking the class to identify the strong sounds and those which may not be pronounced. Elicit ways of writing it in a way which represents its pronunciation. You might arrive at something like this: *wadyuwun?*

4 Dictate the lines of the original poem (Box 8) to the class and ask them to write them down according to what they hear next to the corresponding line in their handout. When saying the lines try to achieve as natural a pronunciation as possible. The students write the lines using the 'spell it as it sounds' system, as with *wadyuwun?* above.

5 Ask pairs to compare both what they've written and how each line might be pronounced.

6 Tell the class that the words are from a poem and give out copies of it (Box 8). Encourage them to compare it with their own versions.

7 Initiate a feedback session to discuss the features of connected speech that they encountered. Examples may include: weak forms *bin* (been) and *um* (them), weakening of /t/ to /d in *goddafew* (got a few); ellipsis of auxiliary verbs and other words *binearlong* (been here long), ellipsis of individual sounds e.g. /d/ – *guluk* (good luck).
8 Ask a willing student to read out the dialogue with you, to remodel the pronunciation.
9 Encourage the students to try out the dialogue again, this time aiming for the new pronunciation.

Extension

Students write their own dialogues using a similar system to that used by the author of 'Fishermen'. These are then displayed around the room. Can the other students work out what is being said?

Box 7

A: Hi there, Mac.
B: Hello Buddy.
A: Have you been here long?
B: A couple of hours.
A: Are you catching any?
B: I've got a few.
A: What kind are they?
B: Bass and carp.
A: Is there any size to them?
B: A couple of pounds.
A: I've got to go
B: Too bad
A: I'll see you around.
B: Yeah, take it easy.
A: Good luck.

Notes

After the initial surprise at being asked to write down what they may see as 'incorrect' English, students often enjoy the challenge of speaking in the very natural way that is posed by this activity. It is important not to be too strict about accuracy of production during stage 9. For some students, missing out words and running others together may seem awkward and confusing, especially if it does not occur in their native language. However, it is an important feature of spoken English and, although not every native or advanced speaker would produce utterances like, *binearlong*?, ´*have ´you ´been ´here ´long?*', where each syllable is given equal stress, is far less likely.

Variation

Give out the original 'Fishermen' poem (Box 8) straight away. Ask for suggestions as to what the first couple of lines mean (i.e. 'Hi there, Mac' and 'Hello Buddy'). Discuss with the class how the poet has written the poem as if it were colloquial speech, emphasising the stressed syllables and running words into one another. Ask the students to go through the poem in pairs, writing a 'translated' version of it. Finally, give out the complete translated version (Box 7) for them to compare their ideas against.

Box 8

Fishermen

Hiyamac.
Lobuddy.
Binearlong?
Cuplours.
Ketchanenny?
Goddafew.
Kindarthay?
Bassencarp.
Enysizetoum?
Cuplapowns.
Igoddago.
Tubad.
Seeyaround.
Yeatakideezy.
Guluk.

Anon

2.4 Stage directions

Outline Students are given a dialogue with the stage directions removed. Their task is to put each stage direction back into the most appropriate place

Focus Inferring speakers' attitudes, emotions and intentions in dialogues

Level Intermediate plus

Time 30 minutes plus

Materials and preparation Choose a short dialogue (up to 15 lines) where a range of emotions are being expressed. See the example below from the television soap opera, *Neighbours*. Prepare a transcript of the dialogue with a stage direction for each line written in brackets (Box 9). Now produce another sheet where the stage directions have been blanked out, and are given as a jumbled list at the bottom (Box 10).

Procedure

1 Give each student a copy of the dialogue with the stage directions at the bottom (Box 10). Ask the class to read it, and then discuss with them who they think the characters are and what the situation is.

2 Ask them to work individually to decide which stage direction should go in each of the spaces.

Box 9

Libby: (*angrily*) I thought I told you I didn't want to see you.
Mike: (*walking towards her*) Until I'd faced up to a few things.
Libby: (*turning away*) So leave!
Mike: (*sitting down*) I have every right to be here. I'm going to stay until you hear me out.
Libby: (*impatiently*) Alright. What?
Mike: (*tenderly*) You're right, Libby. I do sweep things under the carpet, and yes I do have trouble communicating my feelings. I ask you to fit into my life without giving you the time or energy you deserve. But you have to know . . . I'm so in love with you. There's no cover big enough to hide that. Now I'm going to make an effort – a serious, concerted effort. I need to be closer to you Libby.
Libby: (*suspicious*) They're lovely words Mike, but they're just that.
Mike: (*looking at her straight in the eyes*) I mean it, Libby.
Libby: (*looking at him*) Do you really think you can put them into action?
Mike: (*standing up*) Well, I've already made a start. I'm moving in to number 32.
Libby: (*amazed*) What?
Mike: (*smiling*) We're going to be neighbours.

3 When they are ready they compare and discuss their ideas in pairs. Can they agree on the most appropriate way to complete the task?
4 Now ask them to try saying the lines, incorporating the stage directions that they've added. Are there any stage directions that they would like to change as a result?

Extension

Ask different pairs to perform their version of the dialogue to each other.

Variation

If the DVD recording of the scene is available, play the scene after stage 4, so that the class can compare and contrast the original with their own versions.

Box 10

Libby: (   ) I thought I told you I didn't want to see you.
Mike: (   ) Until I'd faced up to a few things.
Libby: (   ) So leave!
Mike: (   ) I have every right to be here. I'm going to stay until you hear me out.
Libby: (   ) Alright. What?
Mike: (   ) You're right, Libby. I do sweep things under the carpet, and yes I do have trouble communicating my feelings. I ask you to fit into my life without giving you the time or energy you deserve. But you have to know . . . I'm so in love with you. There's no cover big enough to hide that. Now I'm going to make an effort – a serious, concerted effort. I need to be closer to you Libby.
Libby: (   ) They're lovely words Mike, but they're just that.
Mike: (   ) I mean it, Libby.
Libby: (   ) Do you really think you can put them into action?
Mike: (   ) Well, I've already made a start. I'm moving in to number 32.
Libby: (   ) What?
Mike: (   ) We're going to be neighbours.

angrily
looking at her straight in the eyes
amazed
smiling
tenderly
sitting down
turning away
standing up
looking at him
impatiently
suspicious
walking towards her

2.5 Authentic versus scripted dialogues

Outline Students contrast an authentic dialogue with one that has been scripted and then create their own authentic-style dialogue

Focus Raising awareness about some common features of authentic speech

Level Intermediate plus

Time 40 minutes plus

Materials and preparation Make enough copies of each of the dialogues such as the ones shown below so that there is one for each student.

Procedure

1. Give out copies of the first two dialogues. Allow the students some time to examine them and work out what the situation is.
2. Ask the class which dialogue they think is an example of an actual conversation (Dialogue B). Working in pairs, students now discuss what features of the dialogue tell them it's authentic.

Box 11

Dialogue A

Shop assistant:	Can I help you?
Customer:	Have you got Peter O'Toole's biography which came out about a month ago?
Shop assistant:	I'll look for it for you. I don't know it myself. (*He types into the computer keyboard.*) Are you sure it's recent?
Customer:	I think so.
Shop assistant:	Do you know the title?
Customer:	No, I don't.
Shop assistant:	Is it a biography or an autobiography?
Customer:	Oh, actually I think it's an autobiography.
Shop assistant:	OK. Well there are two. The most recent one is called *Loitering with Intent: The Apprentice*. Do you think that's the one you want?
Customer:	It might be.
Shop assistant:	Ok, I'll show you where it is.

Box 12

Dialogue B

Shop assistant: Can we help you at all?
Customer: Erm . . . biography by Peter O'Toole that came out in the last month or so, do you know if you've got it?
Shop assistant: Peter O'Toole. I'll just have to search for it. I'm not familiar with it (*he types into the computer keyboard*). You say it's . . . it's a recent one?
Customer: I think it's pretty new, yeah.
Shop assistant: Got no idea of the title at all then?
Customer: No.
Shop assistant: Don't know whether it's autobiography or biography?
Customer: This is it. This is it. I . . . I've got a feeling it's autobiography.
Shop assistant: Autobiography. (*pause*) Right. If it's autobiography there are two.
Customer: Right.
Shop assistant: Erm *Loitering with Intent: The Apprentice*. Would that be it? Does that ring a bell?
Customer: It might = It might well be.[1]
Shop assistant: Erm let me show you.

From the CANCODE Corpus of Spoken English

3 Initiate a feedback session to focus on the issues they raise. Points to highlight may include the following:

Performance phenomena

Hesitation devices (*Erm:* lines 2, 15 and 18)
Repetition (*it's . . . it's: line 6, this is it this is it;* line 11)
False starts (*It might= It might well be* line 17)

Interactional/Interpersonal features

Vague language (*at all*: lines 1 and 8; *or so*: line 3)
Ellipsis (i.e. missing words) (. . . *biography by*: line 2; *Got no idea*: line 8; *don't know*: line 10).

[1] The = symbol indicates a false start.

Heads (i.e. using a noun phrase at the front of a clause to introduce the topic) (*biography by Peter O'Toole that came out in the last month or so, do you know if you've got it*: line 2)
Indirect questions (*Do you know if you've got it*?: line 3, *You say it's a recent one*?: line 5)
Backchannels (*Peter O'Toole*: line 4; *right*: line 14)
Evaluative language (*It's pretty new*: line 7, *I've got a feeling*: line 11)
Idiomatic language (*Does that ring a bell?*: line16)

4 Give out the third dialogue (Dialogue C). Ask the students to rewrite it in pairs, converting it into a more authentic version. They should try to incorporate some of the features outlined in the previous stage.

5 Encourage different pairs to compare and contrast the dialogues they have produced.

Box 13

Dialogue C

Shop assistant:	Can I help you?
Customer:	Do you still have any of that cheese with hazelnuts that was on special offer yesterday?
Shop assistant:	What was it called?
Customer:	I can't remember. It was white and had hazelnuts in it.
Shop assistant:	Have you looked on the shelves?
Customer:	Yes, I have.
Shop assistant:	We've only got what is there. Do you mean the cheese with walnuts?
Customer:	Sorry, yes. I mean walnuts. How much is it?
Shop assistant:	It's £9.50 a kilo.
Customer:	I'll have half a kilo please.

2.6 Dialogue scan race

Outline Students take part in a race to find language items with particular meanings in an extract of authentic dialogue

Focus Raising awareness about the meaning and use of some common language items found in authentic conversation

Level Intermediate plus (the example below is for an advanced class)

Time 40 minutes plus

Materials and preparation Find an extract of authentic conversation, or record and transcribe your own. Prepare a worksheet which asks students to find language items with particular meanings in the text. Alternatively, if using the example below, choose questions from the list which are appropriate to your class. You will need to cut up the question sheet in Box 15 into individual questions and place them randomly and face up on a table in front of the class. Each student will also need a copy of the dialogue.

Procedure

1 Give out the dialogue and ask the students to read it and work out what the gist of the conversation is. Try to develop some discussion about it. Who do they think the two speakers are? What sex are they? How old are they? (They are actually young British women. Speaker 1 is an 18-year-old clerk and Speaker 2 is a 19-year-old student.) Was their behaviour reasonable? Could this kind of thing happen in the students' countries?

2 Organise the class into mixed-ability groups of three or four. One person from each group needs to come up and choose one of the cut up questions on the table and take it back to their group. (If mobility is a problem the teacher can act as 'question deliverer'.) The group should now work together to find the appropriate piece of language from the dialogue and write it next to the question. When they have done one, they show it to you (to check whether or not it's correct) and then take another question. If they can't do a question they can put it back on the table again and take a different one.

3 Stop the activity when they are no more questions left on the table, or when the students seem to have done as much as they can. Check which group has managed to answer the most questions correctly, possibly awarding a prize for the winners.

4 Now reorganise the students so that people from different groups are working together. Encourage them to teach each other the linguistic features which they had picked out from the text.

Extension

Later on in the class, or in a future lesson, give out the question sheet again and ask the class to work in pairs or small groups to try to recall the language item for each one.

Box 14

(S1) Paula goes 'What's all this I hear about you slapping Kevin?' I went 'What?' I goes 'How did you know that?' She goes 'My mother told me.' I went 'Your mum knows?' She goes 'Oh yeah'. And then Kevin came in this morning going 'Oh have you heard what Pat did? Oh I don't think there's any need for that do you?'
(S2) When did you slap him?
(S1) Didn't you= I told you, didn't I?
(S2) No.
(S1) Oh Chris, I musta done.
(S2) When?
(S1) Classic. Frid= Last Friday night when I went out with Sue and Steve from work.
(S2) Yeah.
(S1) And then we saw him in O'Neils and he w= him and Mandy were like all over each other and they were winding me up summat wicked. And he wasn't talking to me. He wouldn't come anywhere near me on the dance floor . . .
(S2) Mm.
(S1) . . . and they were like there all over each other. She knew she was winding me up. She was looking over his shoulder at me and stuff.
(S2) Mm.
(S1) And I thought Oh dear and I before I knew what I was doing I walked over to him and I was giving him a gobful. God knows what I said cos I can't remember. I mean I wasn't drunk I just had like a mental block.
(S2) Yeah.
(S1) And then er I slapped him cos he was getting cocky.
(S2) Oh nice one.
(S1) It was really hard round one side of his face.
(S2) Nice one.
(S1) And then I thought sod this and slapped round the other side of the face. And he's gone and told his mum and his sister and he he reckoned that there was no need for it.
(S2) Excellent.
(S1) I was like 'no need for it?'
(S2) Oh I'm proud of you Pat.

From the CANCODE Corpus of Spoken English

Box 15

1 A slangy expression meaning 'that's good'

---

2 A short form of 'because', common in spoken language

---

3 A slang expression meaning 'a lot' or 'really badly'

---

4 A single word which roughly means 'this situation is very memorable'

---

5 A phrase meaning 'a lapse in memory'

---

6 A useful way of introducing a piece of gossip

---

7 A colloquial expression which means 'kissing and being very affectionate'

---

8 A phrase which means 'annoying me'

---

9 An example of mild swearing

---

10 A verb used commonly in informal spoken language as an alternative to 'says' or 'said'

---

11 A phrase meaning 'without thinking'

---

12 A colloquial way of reporting speech (to replace 'said'), in this case the speaker's own speech

---

13 A word meaning 'thought' or 'estimated'

---

14 A phrase which means being rude or over-confident

---

15 A chunk of language used to show that you have discovered something about somebody, and to ask for more information

---

16 A phrase which means 'I don't know'

---

17 A phrase meaning 'shouting at him'

---

18 An example of language which is deliberately vague

---

19 The name of a pub

---

20 A phrase meaning 'I'm sure that I did'

Answers

1 nice one (line 27)
2 cos (line 26)
3 summat wicked (line 15)
4 Classic (line 11)
5 a mental block (line 24)
6 Oh, have you heard what Pat did? (line 4)
7 all over each other (line 15)
8 winding me up (line 20)
9 sod this (line 30)
10 goes (line 3) – note that the past form (went) and the present participle (going) are also used
11 before I knew what I was doing (line 22)
12 was like (line 34)
13 reckoned (line 31)
14 getting cocky (line 26)
15 What's all this I hear about . . . (line 1)
16 God knows (line 23)
17 giving him a gobful (line 23)
18 and stuff (line 20)
19 O'Neils (line 14)
20 I musta done (line 9)

2.7 Filling in

Outline	Students incorporate discourse markers into a dialogue from which these have been removed
Focus	Encouraging learners to notice the ways in which discourse markers like *anyway* and *though* are used
Level	Intermediate plus
Time	10 minutes plus
Materials and preparation	Prepare two copies of the same dialogue; one including discourse markers and one without them. Alternatively, write it on the board.

Procedure

1 Give out the version of the dialogue without discourse markers (Box 16). Discuss with the class the context in which the dialogue is taking place.

Tell the students that some words have been removed from it. Can they work out what might be missing?

2 Write up on the board the discourse markers which have been removed. (*Anyway, you know, then, right, OK then, I mean, though* and *well* in the case of the dialogue below). Ask the class to work in pairs and to discuss the most appropriate place to include each one.

3 Give out the dialogue with the discourse markers included (Box 17). Discuss with the whole class what effect each one has in the dialogue and whether any alternatives are possible.

Box 16

A: I think we should buy it. It's just what we want, isn't it?
B: It's a lot of money.
A: I know, but I think we can afford it.
B: If you're sure.
A: I'll give them a ring.
B: I've got to go now. Can you phone them from work? I'll speak to you later.

Box 17

A: You know, I think we should buy it. I mean, it's just what we want, isn't it?
B: It's a lot of money though.
A: Well, I know, but I think we can afford it, can't we?
B: OK then, if you're sure.
A: Right, I'll give them a ring then.
B: Anyway, I've got to go now. Can you phone them from work? I'll speak to you later.

Variation

Instead of discourse markers, other groups of language items which could be removed include vague language, evaluative language, question tags, backchannels and hesitation devices.

2.8 Speech acts

Outline	Students match lines of a dialogue with a corresponding label
Focus	Raising awareness about typical language used for different *speech acts* (i.e. the purposes for which utterances are spoken)
Level	Elementary plus
Time	30 minutes plus
Materials and preparation	Make a transparency copy (or paper ones) of a dialogue like the one in Box 18, incorporating a range of speech acts.

Procedure

1. Give out copies of the dialogue or display it on the overhead projector.
2. Ask the students to match each utterance with one of the speech act labels. Tell them that some of the lines contain more than one speech act.
3. Go through the answers with the whole class. As you do this, elicit words or chunks of language which are typical of each speech act. For instance

   Giving a compliment: *Your* (+noun) *looks* (+ adjective)
   Making a suggestion: *Do you want to* (+ verb)

Box 18

Kusret: Hiya Satveer. How are you doing?
Satveer: Oh, not too bad.
Kusret: Your hair looks nice.
Satveer: Thanks very much. I've just had it cut.
Kusret: Listen. Do you want to come for a drink?
Satveer: I'm afraid I can't. I've got too much work to do.
Kusret: You always say that!
Satveer: No I don't.
Kusret: Oh, go on. I'll help you when we get back.
Satveer: Oh alright then, just a quick one.

making an offer	denying	insisting
giving a compliment	accepting	greeting
making an excuse	making a suggestion	refusing and apologising
responding to a compliment	complaining	responding to a greeting

4 Ask the students to work in pairs to script a dialogue which incorporates some of the speech acts that have been focused on.
5 As pairs finish they show their dialogue to a different pair. Can the other pair work out which speech act is represented by each line?

2.9 The teacher does the speaking test

Outline	The students perform a speaking task, and then notice language items used by more advanced speakers performing the same task
Focus	Encouraging students to notice language items used by higher-level speakers
Level	Pre-intermediate plus
Time	30 minutes plus
Materials and preparation	Choose a paired speaking task appropriate to the level of your students. When working with classes that are preparing for a speaking exam this might involve using the practice speaking exam material normally provided with the coursebook. Make a recording of yourself and another proficient speaker performing the speaking task. With lower levels it may be more appropriate to record two speakers whose level is not too far above that of the students in the class.

Procedure

1 Ask students in pairs to practise the oral exam format you have chosen to work with.
2 Play the recording of the more advanced speakers doing the exam. Ask the class to make a note of useful language that the speakers used. Do this yourself too as you are listening.
3 Ask the students to compare what they wrote down and compile a list on the board of items that were noticed either by yourself, or by the students.
4 Students can now redo the exam in the same pairs as stage 1. Is there any of the language that has been focused on that they can now incorporate into their own speech?

Variation

(For monolingual groups only.) Find two native English speakers whose level of the students' first language is similar to the students' level of English. Ask them to perform the speaking task in the students' first language. When you play the recording back to the learners, ask them to identify, and make a note of, the features of their speech which make it sound non-native. Can they draw any conclusions from this about linguistic features of English which are not present in their mother tongue?

2.10 Student dialogue reformulation

Outline	The teacher prepares a reformulated version (i.e. one containing corrections and improvements) of a student-to-student dialogue, and uses this as a context in which to focus on language
Focus	Extending and developing the language items used within a student-created context
Level	Elementary plus
Time	20 minutes in the first class and 30 minutes plus in the second one
Materials and preparation	Audio recording facilities.

Procedure

Lesson 1

1 Brainstorm dialogue scenarios which the students would like to try out in the class. Decide on the most popular one that it would be feasible to do.
2 Ask the learners to improvise the situation in pairs.
3 Find a pair who would be willing to perform their dialogue again in front of the class and have it recorded. Record it as unobtrusively as possible, but close enough so that both voices are being picked up. You may need to test this first.

Two intermediate level Japanese students in a class which chose the context of 'finding a room to rent' produced the following:

Yuri: *Can you tell me about you?*
Kiyoe: *Oh, I have been here for six months. I'm studying English so I don't have a job.*
Yuri: *Oh, how do you get your money? From your parents?*
Kiyoe: *I save all my money because I used to work for . . .*
Yuri: *Oh, I see.*
Kiyoe: *The company. So I have a money. So you don't worry about the my money.*

Yuri: *You can pay monthly?*
Kiyoe: *I don't mind monthly or pay a week.*

(*continues for another 19 turns*)

Lesson 2 (as soon as possible after the previous lesson)

Preparation

Listen to the recording at home and reformulate what was said to make a new dialogue (see below). To produce a coherent text, it will probably be easier if you roughly transcribe the whole conversation first.

These reformulations may take the form of either corrections or improvements. It may well be that there are utterances in the original transcript which require correction since they failed to communicate the intended message. For example, 'Can I eat my room?' (which was greeted with a blank face by Yuri) and 'If you pay monthly you can pay current month pay or . . . and' have been changed to, respectively, 'Can I eat in my room?' and 'Can you pay for each month in advance?'.

This type of activity also provides an ideal framework for introducing language items which may not normally be part of the students' active vocabularies. So, 'To be honest, I don't like cats, but I don't mind if you have a dog' becomes instead, 'Well, to be honest, I'm not very keen on cats but I'm not bothered if you've got a dog'.

Each student will need a copy of the new dialogue.

Yuri: *So, can you tell me a bit about yourself?*
Kiyoe: *Well, I've been here for six months and I'm studying English – so I haven't got a job at the moment.*
Yuri: *I see. So how do you get your money? From your parents, I suppose?*
Kiyoe: *No. I saved it all up actually. I used to work for a big company. I've got plenty of money. There's no need to worry about that.*
Yuri: *OK. Have you got any objection to paying monthly?*
Kiyoe: *Well, I don't mind. I can pay monthly or weekly – whatever you like.*

(*continues for another 19 turns*)

Pick out several chunks of language from the reformulated dialogue that you want the students to focus on. With the example from my group I used:

Can you tell me a bit about . . .
I've got plenty of . . .

Have you got any objection to . . . ?
Oh, that's a relief . . .
I'm not very keen on . . .
I'm not bothered if . . .
I can't stand . . .
Can you please make sure you . . . ?
I'm very worried about . . .
Can you . . . in advance?
Is it OK to . . . ?

Procedure

1 Ask the class to think back to the previous lesson. If more than one day has passed it may be a good idea to ask them to redo the dialogues and thus reactivate the context.
2 Give out the list of sentence heads. For each one ask them to try to suggest continuations that would fit the same context of trying to find a room to rent, and to say which character (Kiyoe or Yuri in my example) could have said each.
3 Give out the reformulated dialogue and ask the class to underline the places where the chunks are used, and to discuss how comfortable they would feel expressing things using these language items.
4 Ask them to practise the new dialogue in pairs.

Extension

Ask the class to memorise the dialogue for homework and to perform it at the beginning of the next class. (See Chapter 4.)

Alternative procedure for longer conversations

Preparation

After the first class, instead of reformulating the entire dialogue, pick out a few utterances to reformulate, and write up these reformulated versions on a worksheet for the students (see the example below). Make a copy of this for each student. This activity is particularly suited to students preparing for exams which include a paired oral discussion task. The worksheet below (Box 19) includes examples which were reformulated from a discussion about differences in eating habits between the students' countries and Britain (a practice oral exam question for the Skills for Life Entry 3 Paper).

1 Ask the class to recall the topic of the conversation that was recorded in the previous class. Can they remember any of the things that were said by either of the two speakers?
2 Give out the worksheet. Ask the students to discuss who they think said each of the utterances on the list.
3 Now play the recording of the dialogue so that the learners can check their answers.
4 Ask the class if they noticed that some of the things were said in a slightly different way on the recording. For instance number 5 was originally expressed as *I think big difference my country food and the England food*. Play the recording again and ask them to make a note of any extra, missing or different words.
5 Initiate a feedback session to discuss what effect the changes made. For instance, with the examples below, neither of the students had originally used the present perfect to express utterance 1 or 2, so this led into a discussion about how this form is used. Utterance 8 had been expressed as *I'm not agree*, and the student remarked that she had never noticed before that other people were saying it differently.

Box 19

Who said the following things? Tania or Maryam?

1 I've been here nearly three years.
2 I've been here for one year and five months.
3 The weather's always changing – every five minutes.
4 What do you think about the food in your country and in England?
5 I think there's a big difference between the food in England and the food in my country.
6 I think English food is healthier.
7 I think in my country the food is healthier.
8 I don't agree with you.
9 You mean in Portugal they don't fry the fish? They bake it in the oven?
10 When you see it on the plate it doesn't look healthy.
11 I prefer making my own meals, more than going to restaurants and take-aways.
12 I don't like junk food.
13 I don't have time to cook so I eat a lot of fast food.
14 I just cook at weekends when I have time.

2.11 Backchannelling

Outline Students tell personal anecdotes to each other, and incorporate backchannel devices into those that they hear

Focus Raising awareness about how backchannel devices (*mm*, *uhum*, *yeah*, *no*, *right*, *oh*, *really?*, *wow!* etc.) are used to show that the listener is following the anecdote

Level Pre-intermediate plus

Time 30 minutes plus

Materials and preparation For homework ask the students to prepare a short personal anecdote or story to tell in the next class. This could be about something that has happened to them or someone that they know. The stories do not need to be very long.

Procedure

1 Ask the students to tell their anecdotes in pairs or small groups.

2 Invite a volunteer to sit with you at the front of the class. Ask them to tell their story to you. As they do this, use backchannels (*Yeah? Uhuh* etc.) and clarification checks (*On your own?*, *Why was that?* etc.) to indicate that you are listening. Ask the class to note everything you say.

3 Elicit from the class the language that they made a note of, and write it on the board. Can they think of any other things that listeners say when listening to an anecdote? Write these up on the board too. Check that everyone understands how the language is used.

4 Reorganise the students so that they can retell their anecdotes to different people. This time the speaker should allow time for backchannels where appropriate and the listener should try to incorporate them. If the anecdotes are long they just tell the beginning.

5 Ask the students to regroup again and retell the anecdotes, this time without any backchannels. How does this feel different?

6 Discuss with the whole class what effect the backchannels have on the telling of the story. Which backchannels are used in the mother tongue(s) of the students? Are they used more or less than in English?

Note

There are cultural differences in the amount that a listener is expected to contribute in a speaker's extended turn. Kyoko Beaumont, a teacher of Japanese in Birmingham, told me how when she first started using the phone in English she was unsure whether people were actually listening to her. This was because the English speakers she was talking to used backchannels far less than Japanese speakers would tend to do.

3 Reproducing and reconstructing

So far this book has focused on the more passive language skills of understanding and analysis. This chapter bridges the gap from the receptive use of dialogues to their productive use, and lays the foundations for dialogues as something to be practised and created. We will explore this aspect further in the chapters that follow.

One task type that bridges the receptive–productive gap is the dictogloss. A basic dictogloss procedure for reconstructing a short dialogue might be as follows:

1 The students listen to a recording of the dialogue or the teacher reads it out.
2 They discuss in pairs what they can remember about it.
3 They listen to the dialogue again and are asked to make a note of the key words used.
4 They work in pairs again, pool the words they wrote down and together write up their best version of the complete dialogue.
5 They are given a written copy of the original dialogue to compare with their own.

An activity like this is a useful one for a number of reasons. Firstly, there is a focus on listening and speaking – students need to understand the dialogue they have heard in order to talk about it or make notes on it, and if they didn't understand certain parts there is a chance that they can be helped towards understanding through discussion with a partner.

There is also an emphasis on writing and accuracy: when students come to write the dialogue down there is an inherent need for them to make it as accurate as they possibly can.

Ideally a task like this also encourages negotiation between students. Because the students work in pairs throughout the exercise, they need to discuss and agree on the suitability of different language items to be included in their dialogue, and this serves the purpose of both encouraging them to use the language items in speech, and focusing clearly on meaning as well as form.

Finally, it is conducive to noticing. When students compare their versions of the dialogue with the original one, they often pick out differences between the two. The process they have been through will make them more open to acquiring the language items which they had been unable to reproduce when writing the dialogue themselves.

The activities in this chapter address some or all of the issues outlined above by asking learners to reproduce and reconstruct a range of different dialogues. The initial activities are very accuracy based, with the later ones requiring more and more creativity on the part of the learners. In the first set of activities, the class are given the complete text of the dialogue they are working with, and need to decide on an appropriate way of organising it. Jumbled lines (3.1), Dialogue rebuilding (3.2), The ultimate gapfill (3.3) and Listen again (3.4) ask the learners to piece together dialogues that they have already heard, while Jumbled reconstruction (3.5) and Dialogue pairs (3.6) focus on constructing new ones.

In Dialogue retranslation (3.7), Retranslated tapescript (3.8) and Dubbing (3.9), the learners compare and contrast dialogues with mother tongue equivalents in order to notice the gap between their ability to express ideas in their first language and their ability to do so in English.

From monologue to dialogue (3.10), Turning news items into dialogue (3.11), Shadow dialogues (3.12) and Mimed dialogues (3.13) involve the learners creating dialogues out of other sources. Modernised voiceovers (3.14) and Roughing up and censoring (3.15) encourage the class to produce alternative versions of dialogues, which are suitable for a different audience than the one that was originally intended.

3.1 Jumbled lines

Outline	The class take part in a competitive race to rearrange the words in lines of a dialogue from the coursebook
Focus	Reviewing and reactivating the language of a dialogue already used in class
Level	Any
Time	20 minutes
Materials and preparation	Rewrite a section of a dialogue which the class have already listened to in a previous lesson, so that the words of each utterance are jumbled up. Intersperse these lines with the original unjumbled lines. (See the example below from *Language in Use – Beginner* (p. 111)) Copy this onto a transparency and find the appropriate place on the tape.

Procedure

1 Organise the students into groups of about three. Ask each group to decide on a name for their team.

2 Explain that they are going to have to unscramble the words of the sentences you reveal to them and to say them in the correct order. Tell them that you will accept the answer from the first person to shout out his or her team's name, and that you will award two points for a correct answer and take away one point for an incorrect answer. Explain that a point will also be deducted if there is too much of a delay between shouting out their team's name and providing an answer.

Box 20

Do you do what so?
So . . . what do you do?
Student I'm oh a.
Oh, I'm a student.
Yes oh. Study do you what?
Oh yes. What do you study?
Music.
Music.
Really? Music I'm a teacher.
Really? I'm a music teacher.
Really are you? Where then you do work?
Are you really? Where do you work then?
School at a Cambridge oh in.
Oh, at a school in Cambridge.
Really? Cambridge live you do in?
Really? Do you live in Cambridge?
Yes. Do I yes. Where do live you why?
Yes. Yes, I do. Why, where do you live?
Cambridge. Live I too in Cambridge.
Cambridge. I live in Cambridge, too.
Really? Where?
Really? Where?
Street in Bridge – have I flat a Bridge in Street.
In Bridge Street – I have a flat in Bridge Street.
Amazing that's no . . .
No, that's amazing . . .

3 Go through the sentences, pulling down a piece of paper on the transparency to reveal one sentence for them to unjumble. Play the relevant bit of the tape as a way of feeding back to learners before revealing the correct version of the sentence below.

Notes

This activity is based on 'Present Perfect Love Story' in *More Grammar Games* (1995) by Mario Rinvolucri and Paul Davis, but has been adapted to focus on oral language.

3.2 Dialogue rebuilding

Outline	Students review a dialogue that they have worked with previously, by reconstructing it in pairs
Focus	Raising awareness about how utterances link together in a dialogue
Level	Any
Time	30 minutes plus
Materials and preparation	Using a dialogue that students have already encountered, rewrite it so that the utterances are in two separate jumbled up lists, one for each character (see the example below from *Messages 3* (*Teacher's Book*) (p. 116). It helps if these lists are done in two different colours. Now cut up each list to make piles of utterances and keep them together with a paper clip. Each pair of students will need two utterance piles (one for each character) and both jumbled up lists.

Procedure

1 Put the class into pairs. Give one character's utterances to one person and the other character's to the other. Allow them time to spread their piles out on the table in front of them.

2 Tell them what the first line of the dialogue is, and ask them to find it and put it down on the table in front of them. Students now take it in turns to put lines from their lists down underneath the first utterance, to try to construct the complete dialogue.

3 When you feel that they've done as much as they can, play the recording or read the dialogue so students can check their answers.

4 Now ask them to put the dialogue they've constructed back into a pile, and give each pair both jumbled up lists. Their task now is to reconstruct the dialogue orally. One student looks at the list for one character, and the other student has the other list. They take it in turns to say their lines in the correct order.

5 Play the dialogue again for students to compare with their own versions.

Variation

If the dialogue is not too challenging and is sufficiently well linked, this activity can also be done with dialogues that the learners have not yet encountered.

Box 21

The complete dialogue

Rosa: Hi, Gary.
Gary: Hi, Rosa. How are you?
Rosa: Great. I've just been canoeing. I went about eight kilometres down the river this morning. Have you ever tried canoeing?
Gary: No, I haven't.
Rosa: I really love it.
Gary: Mmm. Everyone's doing something exciting.
Rosa: What do you mean?
Gary: Well, you know Megan? She's just played in the basketball final.
Rosa: Oh yes, I know. Megan was brilliant.
Gary: Yeah. I think she'll get into the national team one day.
Rosa: Yeah, maybe she will.
Gary: And then there's Jay. He's bought a wetsuit and goggles. He's going to take scuba-diving lessons.
Rosa: Oh, really? Great.
Gary: And I've just seen Tom. He's just done a bungee-jump. I've never done anything interesting.
Rosa: Gary that's rubbish. Your paintings are really good. I think you might win the art prize at school this year.
Gary: Hmm, well, maybe . . .

Box 22

Rosa

Oh, really? Great.

I really love it.

Yeah, maybe she will.

Oh yes, I know. Megan was brilliant.

Hi, Gary.

Great. I've just been canoeing. I went about eight kilometres down the river this morning. Have you ever tried canoeing?

Gary that's rubbish. Your paintings are really good. I think you might win the art prize at school this year.

What do you mean?

Gary

Yeah. I think she'll get into the national team one day.

Well, you know Megan? She's just played in the basketball final.

No, I haven't.

And then there's Jay. He's bought a wetsuit and goggles. He's going to take scuba-diving lessons.

Hmm, well, maybe . . .

Hi, Rosa. How are you?

Mmm. Everyone's doing something exciting.

And I've just seen Tom. He's just done a bungee-jump. I've never done anything interesting.

3.3 The ultimate gapfill

Outline	Students try to reconstruct a dialogue that they have already listened to by using a wordlist and a skeleton text
Focus	Raising awareness about the grammatical and lexical patterns of spoken English and developing intensive listening skills
Level	Any
Time	30 minutes plus
Materials and preparation	You will need to prepare a skeleton text of the tapescript (where each word is represented by a blank line), and a wordlist of all the words which ave been taken out of the dialogue. The example below, uses Exercise 1 from Review 3 of *Activate Your English, Pre-intermediate*.

Procedure

1 After doing the content-focused listening activities in the book, give out the skeleton text and word list and ask the learners in pairs to fill in as much as they can using the words at the bottom, and crossing them off as they go.

2 As they begin to run out of ideas, ask them to sit on their hands (so that they can't write while they listen) while you play the tape again. As the tape finishes tell them to fill in again what they can remember and then share what they've done with a partner. Different students tend to pick up different elements, so it's useful to encourage them to interact as much as possible here. They also need time to process and think about which words are possible, both grammatically and lexically, for each space.

3 Repeat this process until one pair have got all of it, or until you feel they've got as much as they can. Allow them to check with the tapescript at the back of the book while they listen again for the final time.

Notes

This activity is a mixture of 'Cheating dictation' in *Dictation* (1988) by Paul Davis and Mario Rinvolucri and 'Grammar Emergence: Task sheet 1' in *Uncovering Grammar* (2001) by Scott Thornbury. It works much better with fairly short tapescripts.

Variation 1

Ask students to turn their papers over while they listen so that they can't see the skeleton text at all. This increases the level of challenge.

Box 23

Skeleton text

Carmen: ________ ________ ________ ________,
________ ________!

Stranger: ________. ________, ________ ________?

Carmen: ________. ________ ________ ________
________ ________ ________ ________
________? ________ ________ ________
________?

Stranger: ________, ________.

Carmen: ________ ________ ________ ________
________.

Stranger: ________ ________ ________ ________.

Carmen: ________.

Stranger: ________ ________ ________ ________
________ ________. ________ ________
________ ________ ________ ________
________.

Carmen: ________, ________ ________ ________,
________ ________?

Choose where to place the following words in the text to complete the dialogue. You may use each word only once.

before bomb alert yes there's I terrible isn't
failure always the it it we something the
it mmm had there the see what wonder
that leaves train's excuse this yesterday on yeah
track a oh time yeah probably a last again
is maybe signal week I late it's was snow
the that was isn't

The complete dialogue

Carmen:	The train's late again, I see!
Stranger:	Yeah. Terrible, isn't it?
Carmen:	Mmm. I wonder what the excuse is this time? Leaves on the track?
Stranger:	Yeah, probably.
Carmen:	Maybe it's a signal failure.
Stranger:	We had that yesterday.
Carmen:	Oh.
Stranger:	Last week it was the snow. Before that it was a bomb alert.
Carmen:	Yes, there's always something, isn't there?

Variation 2

With very short dialogues, write two copies of the 'skeleton', one on each side of the board. Divide the class into two teams and give each team a complete set of all the words needed for their dialogue, written out on separate pieces of card (preferably a different colour for each team) and some Blu-tack. The students work together in each team to stick the words up in the appropriate places and reconstruct the complete dialogue. The first team to do this is the winner. This works well with service encounters and other more predictable dialogues, e.g.

A: *Who's next?*
B: *Half a kilo of onions, please.*
A: *Anything else?*
B: *No thanks.*
A: *That'll be 75p.*

3.4 Listen again

Outline	Students listen to a dialogue repeatedly, each time attempting to write down more of what is being said
Focus	Developing intensive listening skills and raising awareness about typical spoken utterances
Level	Any
Time	20 minutes plus (depending on the length and the difficulty of the dialogue)

Materials and preparation	Choose a dialogue from the coursebook, or other source, of up to about 15 short turns, and find the relevant section of the recording which goes with it. Prepare a sheet with just the names of the characters in the dialogue down the left hand side, and a space to write in what they say. Each student will need a copy of this sheet plus the complete dialogue.

Procedure

1 Play the recording and ask the students to discuss in pairs what they understood.
2 Now give out the sheet with just the names of the speakers down the side to each student. Play the tape again and ask them to write down what they can understand for each person's line as they hear it. At this stage there will only be time to write down a few words at the most, and they will probably be able to complete more from the beginning than the end of the dialogue. Allow them sufficient time at the end of the recording to continue making notes if they wish to.
3 Encourage students to compare and discuss what they've written down after they've listened, and then play the tape again. Keep repeating this process until you feel that they've done as much as they can.
4 Now give out the complete dialogue and allow them to listen again.

Note

It is important not to use dialogues which are too long or this activity can become demotivating.

3.5 Jumbled reconstruction

Outline	The teacher dictates a series of lines to the students which they then organise into a coherent dialogue
Focus	Useful ways of keeping a conversation going and providing a springboard for the learners' own dialogues
Level	Any (the example below is for an intermediate class)
Time	30 minutes
Materials and preparation	Find or write a short dialogue which incorporates the language area you wish to practise. See the example below.

Procedure

1 Dictate the lines of the dialogue to the students in a random order.
2 Ask them to work together in pairs to compare spellings and to write the dialogue up into the most logical order.
3 Ask them to practise the dialogue in pairs.
4 Encourage them to have their own dialogues starting with the first line (in this case 'Did you have a nice holiday?') and incorporating some of the language from the original. These can be about real or imagined experiences.

Box 24

Did you have a nice holiday?
Brilliant, thanks.
Where did you go?
We went to the north of Scotland.
Oh lovely. I've never been there. What's it like?
Really beautiful! It was a bit cold though.
Were you camping?
You've got to be joking! No, we stayed in a youth hostel.
I bet that was cheap. Who did you go with?
Just me and the kids.
What did you do all the time, then?
Well, we did a lot of walking and went swimming in the sea.
So, it was quite a cheap holiday overall, then.
Yeah, it was, I suppose.

TIP

If you feel that the class may struggle too much with some of the meanings of language items at the dictation phase, then these can be pre-taught beforehand.

Variation 1

Cut up the dialogue into strips (one strip for each line) and give one strip to each student, doubling up on some of the lines if you have more students than lines. Each student has to remember their line exactly. Now ask the class to mingle around. Each time two students meet they should swap lines. They do this by saying their line to each other and then trying to remember the line that they've just heard. They each then move on to someone else and say this new line. This process continues until everyone has worked with at least ten people.

Now ask them to sit down with a partner and to try to reconstruct the dialogue based on their memory of the lines that they swapped. If they feel that there are gaps in the dialogue then they need to create the missing lines. Because of the memory load, this is much more challenging than the procedure outlined above.

Variation 2

Rewrite the utterances in the dialogue as a jumbled list, and pin up copies of this on the wall outside the classroom. Students work in pairs. Student A has to go outside the room, read the list and try to remember one of the utterances. Student A comes back in and says it to their partner. Student B writes down what student A has said. Student A then goes out again to memorise another utterance and then comes back and says that utterance to student B. As student B starts to get a list of utterances written down, and while they are waiting for more utterances from student A, student B tries to rearrange what they have written into a coherent dialogue. This activity is a variation of what has become popularly known as a 'Running Dictation', which I first came across in *Dictation* (1988) by Paul Davis and Mario Rinvolucri, in this series.

3.6 Dialogue pairs

Outline	The students take part in a card game where contexts for short exchanges are found and discussed
Focus	Developing pragmatic awareness and encouraging discussion about the contexts in which dialogues occur
Level	Intermediate plus
Time	15 minutes plus
Materials and preparation	Each group of two to eight students needs a set of lines such as those in Box 25, preferably photocopied onto card and cut up.

Procedure

1 Organise the class into groups of up to eight.

2 This activity is much easier to demonstrate than to explain. Gather the class around one group of students to show them how it works, and join in yourself with this group. These are the rules:

- a The pack of cards is placed face down on the table. Each pair (or individual if you have odd numbers) within the group picks seven cards from the pack.
- b The object of the game is for each pair to win as many tricks as they can before somebody runs out of cards.
- c One pair is chosen to start. They choose one of their cards and place it on the table. Cards using lower case letters can only be used in the second position, but those using capitals can be used either to start or conclude an exchange.
- d The next pair now needs to place down a card which naturally follows on from what is already there. For instance: pair A puts down *I'VE JUST BEEN OFFERED A NEW JOB*, pair B puts down *Congratulations!* And wins the trick. *Congratulations!* or *That's great!* may be the most obvious choices but there are also other possibilities. Pair B could also put down *I'M GOING OUT NOW* as a response. In order to claim the trick they would need to explain the context in which this exchange could happen (for example the second speaker is in a real hurry and doesn't have time to hear the details of the first speaker's good news. Alternatively, they are so shocked by the news that they need to go out and spend some time on their own).
- e If a pair are unable to follow on they must take a card from the pack and miss their turn. If they can't find a context in which the exchange could happen they need to pick up the card again before taking a new card and missing their turn. There will of course be certain cards which cannot be made to fit. For example, it would be very difficult to argue that *Yes, please. It's delicious* could follow *I'VE JUST BEEN OFFERED A NEW JOB*. If students can't agree on whether an utterance fits or not you will need to intervene.
- f It is now the next pair's turn to start a new exchange by putting down a new line which the following pair need to find a response to.
- g When one pair manages to put down their last card, or there are no more cards left in the pack, it is the end of the game, and the pair with the most tricks wins.

3 When you feel that everyone has understood how the game works, give a set of cards to each group and let them play the game.

Box 25

OUCH!
I'VE JUST CUT MY FINGER.
ARE YOU COMING WITH ME?
IT'S HALF PAST EIGHT.
DO YOU WANT A LIFT?
I'VE JUST BEEN OFFERED A NEW JOB.
I'M GOING TO MISS YOU.
IT'S JUST STARTED TO RAIN.
WHERE ARE YOU GOING?
I'M GOING OUT SOON.
WHY DON'T YOU GO TO BED?
LET'S OPEN A WINDOW.
SHALL WE TURN DOWN THE HEATING?
WHERE'VE YOU BEEN?
DO YOU WANT TO GO SWIMMING?
WHOSE IS THIS?
WHAT WOULD YOU LIKE?
ARE YOU GOING TO STAY THERE?
DO YOU WANT SOME MORE?
IS THIS YOURS?
I'M REALLY TIRED.
HAVE YOU GOT A LIGHT?
WHAT'S THE MATTER?
OH NO!
I'M GOING OUT NOW.
IT'S HOT IN HERE.

A cheese sandwich.
How?
Sorry.
Really?
No, sorry.
Congratulations!
That's great!
Me too.
Home.
No thanks. I'm full.
I don't want to.
I can't.
No, it's not.
Yes please. It's delicious.
I might do.
It's mine.
I'm fine thanks.
No. I'm coming back later.
Yeah.
I know.
Nowhere.
No thanks.
Nothing.
Good.
So am I.
I don't know.

3.7 Dialogue retranslation

Outline	Students test each other on their ability to retranslate utterances from mother tongue to English
Focus	Raising awareness about the gap between the students' passive and active levels of English
Level	Any
Time	30 minutes plus
Material and preparation	Choose a dialogue from the coursebook or other source of up to 10–15 lines and which is appropriate to the level of the group. Cut it up line by line and give each student a set.

Procedure

1 Give out copies of the cut up dialogue to individual students. Ask them to write a natural mother tongue translation of each utterance on the back of each slip. Stress that they need to translate the sentences into what people would actually say in their mother tongue, rather than literally, word for word. Encourage access to dictionaries if they need them.

2 Get students to test each other in pairs. One student (the tester) looks at the English version of the utterance. The other student (the tested) looks at the mother tongue version and tries to recall as much as they can of it in English. They both provide clues for each other where necessary and swap roles frequently. If you are working in a multilingual classroom it will obviously only be possible for learners to retranslate utterances which are written in their own mother tongue.

Variation 1

Ask learners to translate the whole dialogue rather than a line at a time. This provides the learners with more contextual clues when they come to translate back, but takes away the element of oral practice.

Variation 2

Delay the translating back stage until several minutes, hours or even days later, after students have been involved in other activities. This way long-term memory is also being activated.

Variation 3

Ask the learners to tick all the parts which they produced correctly and to change the areas where there were differences between their English version and the original one. Tell them to produce sentences which incorporate the language items which were new to them and which they could imagine themselves saying.

Notes

The retranslation technique has been around for a very long time and is an excellent way of raising student-awareness about their active versus passive level of the language they are learning. By using dialogues instead of standard written text this is extended to incorporate spoken as well as written English.

3.8 Retranslated tapescript

Outline	Students translate a section of a tapescript into their mother tongue, retranslate it back into English in the next lesson, and then compare their translations with the original English version
Focus	Raising awareness about the gap between the students' passive and active levels of English
Level	Elementary plus
Time	20 minutes of class time (more for homework)
Materials and preparation	Each student needs a copy of the tapescript of a listening text which you have been working on in class. This activity works best with quite short extracts which are not too far above the active language level of the students (it may not be appropriate to use the whole transcript).

Procedure

1 After doing a coursebook listening exercise give out a copy of the dialogue to each student, or direct their attention to the tapescript at the back of their books.

2 Ask them to translate the section you have chosen into their mother tongue for homework. Stress that they should translate the message of what is being said rather than word for word.

3 In the next class make sure the learners can only see their mother tongue version and not the original English version. Ask them to orally retranslate it back into English. Do this in pairs first so that learners can bounce ideas off each other. Monitor this stage carefully.

4 Go through the translation with the whole group, calling on individuals who produced competent English versions in the pairwork to do the same in front of everyone. After each sentence or utterance play the relevant part of the tape so that students can check their work.

Note

There will be differences between what students say in the final feedback and what is on the tape. It may well be that there are many appropriate ways of saying the same thing. This can be brought up and discussed in feedback.

3.9 Dubbing

Outline	Learners dub the lines of a dialogue onto a silent viewing of an excerpt from a film or soap opera
Focus	Raising awareness about the gap between the learners' level of English and a more advanced level
Level	Pre-intermediate plus
Time	20 minutes plus (depending on the length of the scene chosen)
Materials and preparation	Choose a short dialogue from a film or soap opera in English which will be of interest to your group. Each student needs a copy of this dialogue. You will also need the DVD recording of the scene that goes with it.

Procedure

1 Hand out copies of the script to the students. Encourage them to read it, and check with them any issues of meaning or pronunciation.
2 Play the scene for students to watch (several times if necessary).
3 Now turn down the sound. Ask the students to work in groups which are the same size as the number of characters in the scene. Each student takes one of the roles. Ask them to read the script to fit in with the actors.
4 Play the scene again and ask one group to perform their version for the rest of the class.
5 Play the scene with the sound turned up again. What differences do the students notice?

Variation 1

Don't give out the script. After playing the scene a few times ask the students to try to write out their own reconstructed version of it. They now dub the film using their own text. Now play the original version again.

Variation 2

Prepare a translation of the scene into the mother tongue of the class (only suitable for monolingual groups). Give this out to the students and ask them to work together to translate it into English. They then dub this version onto the scene, before finally watching the original English version.

Variation 3

Show a scene to the students in their mother tongue (several times if necessary). Ask them to try to write an English version of it. They then dub this onto the film.

3.10 From monologue to dialogue

Outline	The class convert a monologue back into dialogue format, and then compare it with the dialogue that it was originally converted from
Focus	Encouraging students to notice the linguistic features which help to make interaction more dialogic
Level	Any (this example is for an elementary group)
Time	30 minutes plus
Materials and preparation	Find a dialogue from your coursebook where the listener is clearly reacting to the speaker's lines, and convert it into monologue format. Make a copy of this and the original dialogue for each student. (See the example in Box 26 overleaf, which has been converted from Recording 68 in *Wavelength – Elementary*.)

Procedure

1 Give out copies of the monologue to the group. Read it out to the class without pausing. Ask them how they would feel if a friend of theirs interacted with them in such a way. Discuss how usually, when one person is talking, the other person makes comments and asks questions about what has been said, and this helps to make the conversation flow more smoothly.

2 Start converting the monologue back into a dialogue on the board with the whole group. Use the first few lines of the original tapescript (Box 27) to get them on the right track and illustrate a few examples of the kind of questions and comments that the listener needs to make.

3 Ask students to continue converting the monologue into dialogue format in pairs.

4 Ask one or two pairs to read out their dialogue to the rest of the class.

5 Play the original recording of the dialogue. Ask students to make a note of any useful language which the listener used to show interest and keep the conversation going.

6 Give out the original tapescript and encourage the students to notice any language that they had previously missed.

Box 26

This weekend some good things and some bad things happened. The good news is that I finally passed my driving test. I drove the family to the beach on Sunday. We had some problems though. The traffic was terrible. It was awful, really awful. It was very, very hot.

It took us six hours to get there! We finally got there and we found a lovely little beach. It was beautiful, really beautiful. Then it started to rain so we ran back to the car.

Box 27

Will: Did you have a good weekend?
Rose: Well, yes and no . . .
Will: Why? What happened?
Rose: Well, first the good news. I finally passed my driving test.
Will: Congratulations! That's great!
Rose: Yeah, thanks. I drove the family to the beach on Sunday.
Will: That sounds nice.
Rose: Yeah, but we had some problems.
Will: What sort of problems?
Rose: Well . . . the traffic was terrible!
Will: Oh, no!
Rose: Oh yeah! It was awful, really awful. It was very, very hot.
Will: Oh, I know. It was terrible yesterday.
Rose: Anyway . . . It took us six hours to get there!
Will: You're joking! Six hours?!
Rose: Yes. Anyway, we finally got there and we found a lovely little beach. It was beautiful, really beautiful.
Will: Yeah?
Rose: And then it started to rain.
Will: Oh, no!
Rose: So we ran back to the car, and . . .

3.11 Turning news items into dialogue

Outline The class experiment with converting news items into dialogue and vice versa

Focus Raising awareness about differences between dialogic and monologic forms of language, and developing writing skills

Level Intermediate plus

Time 40 minutes plus

Materials and preparation Find two short quirky news stories and label these 'Story A' and 'Story B' (see the 'News in Brief' section in the *Guardian* or www.ananova.com or www.metro.co.uk for further examples), and for each one prepare a short dialogue which expresses the same information as the story. See the examples below.

Procedure

1 Divide the class into two fairly equal groups. Give the first group story A and the dialogue version of story B. Meanwhile the second group get story B and the dialogue version of story A (see below).

2 Working in pairs within the two groups, the students' task is to produce a news story based on the information in their dialogue, and a dialogue based on the information in their news story.

3 As they finish, ask them to work with a pair from the other group. Ask them to swap what they've written and compare and discuss differences with the originals.

Story A

A Coventry couple have won a competition on the most unusual place to fall in love. He was a dustman collecting her rubbish and she was rummaging in her bin searching for lost car keys. *Coventry Evening Telegraph*, 4 *October 2000*

Story B

A walker in Todmorden, West Yorkshire, had to flee from a barn in his underwear when he set light to his clothes and the barn after sheltering there from torrential rain. *Yorkshire Post, 28 September 2000*

Box 28

Dialogue A

A: So how did you two meet, anyway?
B: Well . . . It's quite unusual.
A: Yeah?
B: I'd been looking for my car keys all over the place. I couldn't find them anywhere and was getting pretty desperate. I ended up outside, rummaging through the dustbin to see if I'd dropped them in there by mistake.
A: Wow! You must have been desperate!
B: And then Mike turned up. He was working as a dustman at that time and he wanted to empty my bin.
A: And you got talking?
B: Yeah . . . and that was it! Do you know we even won this competition a few years back on the most unusual place to fall in love.

Dialogue B

A: Did you have a good walk this afternoon?
B: No, I didn't!
A: Why? What happened?
B: Well to start with, it absolutely poured down with rain.
A: Yeah. I was going to say . . .
B: And then I was sheltering in this barn to try and dry off, and I lit a fire to try and get my clothes dry.
A: That was lucky that there was a barn . . .
B: And then my clothes and the barn caught fire, and I had to make a run for it.
A: Oh God! You're joking!

3.12 Shadow dialogues

Outline	The class listen carefully to each other's conversations and try to produce a written version of them
Focus	Raising awareness about learners' own language use during discussions. Developing intensive listening skills
Level	Elementary plus
Time	40 minutes plus
Materials and preparation	None.

Procedure

1 Put students into groups of four, five or six. Ask them to decide on a roleplay situation or a discussion which could keep them talking for about a minute. With lower levels it may be more appropriate to give them some suggestions. Some examples might be: a nice place to go on holiday, the best way to learn English, arranging an evening out, or discussing whether or not hospitals should be free.

2 If they're in a group of four, two people have the discussion while the other two sit behind each speaker and listen carefully to what their speaker says. They may make notes but, since the speakers will be talking at normal speed, they won't have enough time to write down the exact words that were spoken. With groups of five, have two speakers and two shadows for one of the speakers. With groups of six, have three speakers and three shadows.

3 Swap the roles around so that everyone gets a chance to be a speaker and a shadow.

4 The two or three shadows for each conversation now come together and try to produce a written dialogue which is as close as possible to what was originally said by the speakers. If it's too much to write everything, ask them to write a dialogue which summarises the main things that the speakers said. Are there any improvements that could be made to the final version without changing the intended meaning? Any necessary changes are made at this stage.

5 Shadows then present the dialogues to the class, trying to sound as much as they can like the original speakers. The original speakers then comment on how different or similar the shadow dialogues were to their own.

6 Each pair receives a copy of their own shadow dialogue. They read it and discuss any differences that they notice.

Notes

This activity works particularly well when there is a difference in level between speakers and shadows. If the speakers' language skills are higher, then the shadows are nicely challenged to process language which is more advanced than they would normally use themselves. On the other hand, if the shadows are more competent speakers, then they provide some useful and non-threatening reformulations of the speakers' utterances.

Variation

Ask another teacher to come into your class to ask you about something, or take a call on your mobile phone. Now ask the students to write down as much as they can of the dialogue (with the mobile phone version, they will need to imagine what the other person was saying). Students can then perform their dialogues to the rest of the class and discuss which is closest to the original. Of course this activity can also be used as a follow-up to unsolicited interruptions or phone calls.

3.13 Mimed dialogues

Outline	Students present mimed versions of dialogues to each other and then try to write up the dialogue they have observed
Focus	Encouraging physicalisation, noticing and activation of typical spoken utterances
Level	Elementary plus
Time	30 minutes
Materials and preparation	Make enough copies of dialogues similar to the ones in Box 29 so that each pair of students has one dialogue. You need to use at least three different dialogues.

Procedure

1 Choose one of the dialogues yourself. Working with one confident student, present the dialogue to the rest of the class without speaking, but through mime and gesture. As you do this write up their suggestions for each line on the board. Now give out the original dialogue so that they can compare it with the dialogue on the board.
2 Give each pair one of the other dialogues. Ask them to work out how they could present it through mime, and then to practise it in their pairs.
3 Now organise the class so that each pair is working with another pair with a different dialogue.
4 Ask them to present their mimed versions of the dialogues to each other. They may need to perform the dialogues twice. Those who are watching need to observe carefully and think about what the mimes might mean.
5 Each pair now has the task of trying to write the dialogue for the mime that they just saw.
6 Ask them to get together with the pair that they worked with before, share what they wrote and compare it with the original dialogue.

Variations

Instead of just miming, students can perform their dialogues using gibberish as well (see Gibberish scenes (8.3)) or, in a multilingual class, in their first languages.

Box 29

A: What shall we do after lunch?
B: Do you want to play tennis?
A: I can't. My arm still hurts.
B: OK. Let's stay in and watch television.
A: What's on?
B: I think there's some rugby on later.

A: Will you help me with the washing up?
B: I can't. I'm going out.
A: Where are you going?
B: Ice skating.
A: Are you going to walk there?
B: No. I'm going on the bike.

A: Do you want to play chess?
B: No, it's boring.
A: Well, what do you want to do then?
B: Let's go for a picnic.
A: It's too cold.
B: Well, put your coat on.

A: Would you like a cup of tea?
B: Yes, please.
A: And a piece of cake?
B: No, thanks. I'm on a diet.
A: Are you? You should come for a run with me.
B: I can't. I haven't got time.

A: Did you catch any fish?
B: Yes, four.
A: How big are they?
B: Not very big.
A: Shall we cook them in the oven?
B: No, it's better to fry them.

Notes

It is unlikely that students will write dialogues which are exactly the same as the originals. This doesn't matter. In fact, more negotiation tends to happen if there is a difference in opinion about how the dialogue should be interpreted, and this may also lead them to notice more language at the final comparison stage.

3.14 Modernised voiceovers

Outline	The class rewrite a dialogue to make it more up-to-date in terms of language, and use it as a voiceover for the film it was taken from
Focus	Providing practice in planning natural spoken language
Level	Intermediate plus
Time	30 minutes plus
Materials and preparation	You will need a short dialogue from a film which incorporates archaic language (see the example below from *The French Lieutenant's Woman* by Harold Pinter) and, if available, the DVD of the same extract. Other sources include filmed versions of novels by authors such as Jane Austen and Charles Dickens.

Procedure

1 Give out the dialogue to each pair of learners and play the relevant section of the DVD. Discuss how it is set in the past and that the language used is different from how things might be expressed today.

2 Ask them to work together to rewrite it in more modern language. Help them out with language as they need it. They should try to keep the length of the utterances as close as possible to those of the original.

3 Ask some of the pairs to perform their version for the rest of the class. Play the scene on the DVD with the sound turned down, and ask one pair to use their new dialogue as a voiceover for the film extract.

Note

As long as the new utterances remain more or less the same length as the original ones, then it will still be possible to superimpose them onto the DVD version of the scene.

Variation

Instead of using film scripts, students can be asked to modernise dialogues from old-fashioned coursebooks. The dialogue in Box 31 is from *Daily Dialogues: Colloquial English as Spoken by the Educated Classes in England*, by Herbert M. Carr, revised by Will Potter, Berlin: Marburg, 1938, pp. 66–67.

Box 30

Charles: Ernestina, it cannot have escaped your notice that it is fully six weeks since I came down here to Lyme from London.
Ernestina: No. It has not escaped my notice.

Charles clears his throat

Charles: I came to Lyme to explore the flint beds of the Undercliff, to look for fossils – but I have stayed for you.
Ernestina: Ah!
Charles: For your sweet company.
Ernestina: Thank you.
Charles: I am here this morning to enquire if you would allow me to ask your father . . . for your hand.

She looks at him

Ernestina: Yes. I would allow it.
Charles: (*with a smile*) Mind you, I don't know that he approves of me. After all, I don't do what he considers to be work.
Ernestina: Are you suggesting that it is entirely Papa's decision?
Charles: Oh no. It is yours.
Ernestina: Yes. It is. Papa will do what I want.
Charles: In that case . . . might you take pity on a crusty old scientist, who holds you very dear . . . and marry me?

Ernestina bursts into tears

Ernestina: Oh Charles! I have waited so long for this moment.

He takes her hand

Box 31

A jolly, little game of ping-pong

Mr. and Mrs. Irving, with their children, and Mr. and Mrs. Long, are just finishing their dinner at half past eight. Outside the rain patters furiously against the window panes.

Mrs. I: What a terrible night! I'm glad we're all safe and snug at home, and not out motoring.

Mrs. L.: No, there isn't much pleasure in motoring through a violent rainstorm, still less through a snowstorm. What do you propose doing tonight?

Mr. I.: What do you young people say? What would you like to do?

Eric: Hilda was remarking only yesterday we hadn't played ping-pong for donkey's years.

Mrs. I.: That's a good idea. Let's have a game of table tennis. Are you all agreed? (*The other members having expressed their willingness, they go into the children's schoolroom, where the ping-pong table is quickly made ready, the net stretched across and tightened, and rackets and balls put out.*)

Mr. I.: Who's going to play first? Shall we toss for it? (*They toss, and Hilda and Eric start the first game of a net of three, with 21 points to a game.*)

Hilda: That was a let ball, Eric. We don't count that.

Eric: Now we're 3:2. Change service.

Hilda: I find the light rather dazzling.

Eric : (*gallantly*) Come and play at this end, then. It'll be easier for you. (*They change ends, and Hilda finds she can play much better.*)

Mrs. L.: Bravo, Eric! You just hit the ball in time. (*Hilda gives a cry of dismay as she misses a very easy ball.*)

Mrs. I.: Never mind, Hilda, better luck next time.

Mr. I.: Put a twist on your balls, Hilda. (*Hilda follows out her father's suggestion, to Eric's great discomfiture.*)

Mrs. I.: You'll certainly win the next tournament, Hilda.

Hilda: I hope so.

Mr. I.: You spoon your balls too much, Eric. Put your thumb behind your racket, and play backhand. You'll be able to give more of a punch to your shots. What's the score now?

Hilda: Twenty: twenty. We're deuce.

Eric: The deuce we are!

3.15 Roughing up and censoring

Outline	Students convert scenes to make them more suitable for a different audience
Focus	Raising awareness about the features of different dialogue genres and encouraging creative language use
Level	Upper-intermediate plus
Time	50 minutes plus
Materials and preparation	Find two dialogues from films, plays or television which belong to two clearly different genres, plus, if available, the DVD recordings of the scenes. Two such different dialogues might include a script from a children's television programme like *Bob the Builder* (see Box 32) and an excerpt from a gangster film like *Pulp Fiction*.

Procedure

1 Give out the two dialogues (or, if using the DVD, play the two scenes to the student first). Ask them to identify what kind of audience each scene is aimed at, and what the typical features of the dialogues are.

2 Ask them what would happen if the audiences were swapped around. How could they adapt the scenes to make them more suitable? What kind of things would they need to change?

3 Tell half of the class to work on one of the dialogues, and the other half to work on the other one. Their task is to work in pairs and rewrite their dialogue to make it more in line with the style of the other scene. This may involve adapting lines or changing them completely. With the examples given here the *Pulp Fiction* scene could be modified so that the swearing is removed and the speakers are more polite to each other. The *Bob the Builder* dialogue could be changed so that they are less polite, and use more informal language and slang. The students should try to keep the length of the utterances in their new scenes roughly the same as in the original.

4 Ask the students to perform their new dialogues to each other. If using the DVD, students can read their dialogues to fit in with a silent viewing of the film (see Modernised voiceovers (3.14)).

Box 32

***Bob the Builder*: 'Wendy's Busy Day'**

Bob: (*talking to the cat*) I'm sorry Pilchard. I know you want your breakfast but . . .
(*Wendy comes in*)
Wendy: Goodness Bob! You look awful!
Bob: I am ill. I've got a really bad cold.
Wendy: You'd better stay indoors then and keep warm.
Bob: Oh I can't do that. We've got a big resurfacing job to do on the main road.
Wendy: You're not well enough Bob.
Bob: But my machines are waiting for me.
Wendy: Well, I'll tell them you're ill.
Bob: Wendy! All the town's traffic has been redirected so that we can do the job today. It has to be ready before 5 o'clock. Oh dear I feel all dizzy.
Wendy: Oh well, Bob. Why don't I go out with the machines?
(*Bob coughs*)
Wendy: Either the work gets done with me supervising, or it doesn't get done at all.
(*Bob sneezes*)
Wendy: Good, right, I'll tell the machines.
Bob: Take the mobile phone.
Wendy: Of course.

4 Memorising

The importance of memory in learning a second language cannot be underestimated. Just think of how many words a student needs, for both recognition and production, in order to achieve even an intermediate level of English: current estimates put this figure at around 3,000. All of these words, at some time, have to be stored in the student's long term memory, and have to be available for immediate retrieval. But it's not just words that the student needs to commit to memory. Researchers are now convinced that fluency in speech and writing owes in large part to the learner's capacity to store, not just individual words, but lexical 'chunks'. Chunks are groups of words that tend to occur together, either because they are common collocations, like *fair hair*, *fair enough*, *fair and square*, or because they are fixed formulaic utterances, like greetings (*nice to meet you*) and other speech acts (*would you like a cup of tea?*). These chunks are encountered, stored and retrieved as individual units. Some researchers estimate that proficient speakers have a memorised 'bank' of literally tens of thousands of these items.

Dialogues are an ideal way of providing learners with a rich diet of words and chunks in context, and in a format that allows easy and repeated practice. It follows, then, that there are good grounds for sometimes asking students to memorise them.

There are many factors which will influence how readily language items will be retained by students. Repetition is perhaps the most fundamental. The more often the student encounters and repeats a language item, the greater the chance of it being remembered. But this does not mean simply memorising and parroting a dialogue meaninglessly. Memory is aided if the learner is challenged to retrieve the item in new and unusual ways. Being challenged to remember the lines of a dialogue without seeing it (perhaps in a subsequent lesson) is one way of doing this. Turning the activity into a game or competition adds an extra incentive. Redeploying memorised chunks in new contexts and to express personal meanings also contributes to the process of constant recycling and review.

Memory of a word or phrase is also enhanced if it has strong associations. These associations may be emotional. Dialogic utterances tend to be tied very closely to feelings, and the more we can encourage learners to engage with the feelings behind the language, as actors learning lines do, the more readily the memorising strategies of the learners will come into play.

Who said what? (4.1), Reduced dialogues (4.2) and Story to dialogue (4.3) explore ways of challenging learners to recall and reconstruct dialogues that have already occurred.

In Adjacency pair turnover cards (4.4), Remembering the questions (4.5) and Dialogue halves (4.6) the emphasis is on using memorised utterances to create new dialogues.

Line by line (4.7) and Prompts (4.8) move into work with longer dialogues, and look at some techniques used by actors to remember the lines of their scripts.

4.1 Who said what?

Outline	Students mingle around using sentences which practise a particular area of language. They then try to remember the sentences of the others in the class
Focus	Providing controlled language practice in a challenging and motivating way
Level	Elementary plus
Time	20 minutes plus, depending on the number of students
Materials and preparation	Write out some natural sample sentences which include the grammatical or lexical area that you wish to practise and cut them up into individual slips. You need enough for one for each student in the class. The examples below, using the past simple, are for an elementary group. Other areas that lend themselves to this activity include *I'm going to* + verb, *I used to* + verb, *I have to* + verb etc.

I went to a restaurant	I went to a nightclub	I did some ironing
I played football	I was on the phone	I cooked dinner
I went to the cinema	I studied English	I washed my car
I read a book	I listened to some music	I went on the internet
I stayed at home	I cleaned my house	I wrote some emails
I watched TV	I bought a new car	I went for a walk
I went shopping	I went for a drink	I went to bed early

Procedure

1 Give out one slip to each student. Ask them to remember exactly what it says and then put the piece of paper in their pocket.

2 Tell them to mingle around, asking each other questions to elicit what it says on their pieces of paper (with this example the question would be simply 'What did you do last night?'). Each time the question is answered they should ask one or two further questions to get more information. The other person should invent the answers and be as creative or as realistic as they want to. They should try to remember as much as possible about who did what. For example:

A: *What did you do last night?*
B: *I went to a restaurant.*
A: *Who with?*
B: *Britney Spears.*
A: *What did you eat? etc.*

3 Ask them to come back to their seats and to work with the person next to them. They should now try to talk about all the people in the class with their partner, remembering as much detail as possible. For example:

A: *Chool-Son went to a restaurant with Britney Spears and had fish and chips.*
B: *Yes, and Roman watched . . .*

Note

Emphasising that students should be as creative as possible with their answers may help to make what people have said much more memorable for the others.

4.2 Reduced dialogues

Outline	The class try to recall a dialogue that has previously been focussed on, using prompts on the board. (See also Dialogue Building 6.2)
Focus	Reactivating the language of a dialogue
Level	Any
Time	10 minutes plus
Materials and preparation	None.

Procedure

1 Write up the dialogue to be reviewed on the board so that each utterance is represented by just one or two words. (See the example below from *English 365 (Student's Book)* (p. 80, CUP 2004)
2 Elicit from the class what they think each of the words represents from the dialogue.

Box 33

The original version

A: So this is your office. I hope you don't mind sharing.
B: Not at all. I'm used to it!
A: Fine. And you can use this computer. It's connected to the internet.
B: Thanks. Do I need a password?
A: Yes, just type 'visitor' for user name and password.
B: And how about the phone?
A: You just press '1' for an outside line.

The reduced version

A: . . . office . . . mind sharing.
B: . . . at all . . . used . . . !
A: fine . . . computer . . . internet
B: thanks . . . password?
A: Yes . . . 'visitor' . . .
B: . . . phone?
A: . . . press '1' . . . outside . . .

3 Ask pairs to perform the dialogue together, using the words on the board as prompts.
4 Swap the roles around.
5 Rub out the prompts from the board and ask them to try out the dialogue without them.

4.3 Story to dialogue

Outline	The students are helped to remember the dialogue from a story told by the teacher, and then asked to perform it
Focus	Encouraging activation of the dialogue contained in a story
Level	Any (the example below is for an elementary group)
Time	30–40 minutes
Materials and preparation	Choose a story to tell the class which incorporates dialogue and is suitable for their level and interests.

Procedure

1 *Tell* the class the story (rather than reading it to them), making plenty of eye contact with the learners so that you can gauge how well they are following what you are saying.
2 Ask them to work in pairs and to write up the dialogue of the story as a script. You may need to elicit the first line and write it up on the board first.
3 Students now try performing their scripts.
4 Ask them to redo the dialogues without looking at their scripts.

Variation 1

With a more competent group, ask the students to go straight into performing the dialogue between the characters after stage 1 (omitting the writing stage).

Variation 2

Prepare a simple cut up summary of the story (see Box 34). After hearing the story, the students organise the summary into the most logical order. The order is then checked with everybody together and the summaries taken away. The students are then asked to write the script, as above.

Variation 3

Prepare a list of all of the utterances which are said in the story (see Box 35). After telling the story, elicit the names of the characters and write them on the board. In the example used here this would simply be the woman from the village and Nasreddin. Read out the items from your utterance list in a random order. Ask the class to shout out which character said each of the lines. Ask the students to work in pairs. Give one person in each pair the utterances sheet and ask them to test their partner on who said each line. Now take the utterance sheets away again and ask them to write the script.

Box 34

b Nasreddin was walking in the desert. He came to a small village.
d A woman from the village ran up to him. 'Please help us!' she said, 'it hasn't rained in our village for a very long time. We are very thirsty. Our animals are dying. We need water.'
a Nasreddin thought for a moment. 'OK', he said, 'Please bring me a bucket of water.'
c The woman went to get a bucket of water.
e When she came back Nasreddin took off his shirt and started washing it in the water.
g The woman was very angry. 'What are you doing??!!' she shouted. 'You're using our water to wash your shirt. You're crazy!!!'
h Nasreddin didn't listen. He washed his shirt and put it on the washing line to dry.
f Suddenly it started to rain.
i The woman from the village was very happy. 'It always rains when I wash my shirt and put it on the washing line to dry', said Nasreddin.

Box 35

Please help us.
It hasn't rained in our village for a very long time.
We're very thirsty.
Our animals are dying.
We need water.
OK.
Please bring me a bucket of water.
What are you doing??!!
You're using our water to wash your shirt.
You're crazy!!!
It always rains when I wash my shirt and put it on the washing line to dry.

Note

Storytelling provides an ideal format in which to present the language of dialogues to learners. The teacher can model intonation and stress patterns, provide visual clues to aid comprehension, and go over certain bits again where necessary. Variations 2 and 3 above provide extra support, and maximise the potential for the learners to remember, and consequently activate, the language used in the original telling.

4.4 Adjacency pair turnover cards

Outline	Students learn a set of adjacency pair questions and answers by working through a pile of turnover cards
Focus	Adjacency pairs (typical question and answer type utterances). These may include for example, greetings (*How are you doing? – Not too bad*), requesting and accepting (*Will you give me a hand? – Alright*) or typical service encounter scripts (*Have you got any lemons? – No sorry we've sold out*)
Level	Any (the example below is for a beginners class)
Time	10 minutes plus
Materials and preparation	Make a set of turnover cards like those in Box 36 for each pair of students. The cards need to be photocopied so that each answer is on the back of its corresponding question, and then cut up into sets and paperclipped together.

Procedure

1 Give each pair a set of the cards. Students arrange them so that they are in a pile with the answers facing upwards.

2 Ask them to go through all the cards one by one. Their task is to work out what the question is that goes with each answer. They should say it out loud and then turn the card over to check. If they really have no idea what the question is, they turn over the card to have a look.

3 Students go through the cards (several times if necessary) until they can remember what all the questions are without looking at the other side.

4 Ask the learners to interview their partner using the questions they have learnt, adapting them where necessary.

Variation

These materials can also be used to play a form of Pelmanism. For this version of the game, the cards are photocopied with just one utterance on one side. Each pair of students receives one set of cards, which they arrange face down on the table. Students take it in turns to turn over two cards. If they show two utterances which go together, they keep them. If the utterances don't go together, they turn them back over again and put them back in the same place. Gradually students start to remember the position of the utterances they need in order to complete pairs. The student with the highest number of pairs at the end is the winner.

Box 36

Nice to meet you.	Nice to meet you too.
How are you?	Fine thanks.
Do you want some coffee?	Yes please.
Are you hungry?	No, I've just had lunch.
What's your first name?	It's David.
What's your surname?	It's Beckham.
How do you spell your surname?	B-E-C-K-H-A-M
What's your job?	I'm a footballer.
Where do you live?	In Madrid.
Where are you from?	I'm from London.
What's your telephone number?	It's 30165 278596.
What's your email address?	It's davidbeckham@cambridge.org
What languages do you speak?	English and Spanish.
How old are you?	I'm 32.
Are you married?	Yes, I am. My wife's called Victoria.
What's your wife's job?	She's a singer.
Do you have any children?	Yes, I have three. Brooklyn, Romeo and Cruz.
How old are your children?	Eight, five and two.
What did you do yesterday?	I played football.
What are you doing tomorrow?	I'm playing football.

4.5 Remembering the questions

Outline The students learn a series of questions by heart and then ask them of their peers

Focus Fixing questions that activate a particular language area into short-term memory. The example below focuses on common collocations with *make*

Level Any

Time 20 minutes plus

Materials and preparation Prepare two lists of questions which use the language point you wish to practise. Half the class will need one list and the other half will need the other. See Boxes 37 and 38 for examples.

Procedure

1. Divide the class into two sides. Give one side the first half of the questions (Box 37), and the other side the other half (Box 38).
2. Tell them to ask each other the questions and compare answers in pairs. Make dictionaries available and help out with issues of meaning.
3. They now need to choose people from the other side of the class whom they would like to ask each question. Tell them to write down a list of the names of the people they choose on a separate piece of paper. As they will not be able to take the question sheet with them when they ask, they will need to remember exactly which question goes with which person. Demonstrate how they might do this by taking the first question as an example, and talking them through a mental image you have created which links the question with the name of one person in the class. The more striking the mental image created the easier it will be to remember. For instance, imagining the first person on the list jumping out of bed, making their bed at breakneck speed, and then standing to attention like a soldier, should serve to make the first question memorable.
4. When they have gone through all of the questions in this way, ask them to put away the question sheet and to test themselves by just looking at their lists of names and trying to remember the question for each person.
5. Taking only their lists of names with them, the students now mingle around asking their questions and answering any that are asked of them.

Extension

Afterwards, or in the next lesson, pair the students up and ask them to try to recall and discuss which questions they asked to which student and how the student responded.

Variation

Instead of giving out the lists of questions, ask the students to design their own ones from a list of the language items you'd like them to practise, for example: *make your bed*, *make a mess*, *make fun of you*, etc.

Box 37

1 Do you make your bed as soon as you get up?
2 Who makes the most mess in your house?
3 Do people ever make fun of you?
4 What do you think is the best way of making a lot of money?
5 Do you enjoy making up stories?
6 Are you good at making cakes? Do you know somebody who is?
7 Do you feel that you're making progress with your English?
8 Do you make more mistakes when you're speaking or when you're writing?
9 Do you make more effort in the mornings or in the afternoons?
10 Does anyone make a fuss in your house if you come home late?

Box 38

1 Who makes the most noise in your house?
2 Do you find it hard to make decisions?
3 What plans have you made for next year?
4 How many phone calls do you make a day?
5 What kind of things make you angry?
6 When was the last time you had to make an appointment? What was it for?
7 Do you know someone who is always making promises and then not keeping them?
8 Who usually makes dinner in your house? How would you feel if you had to make dinner every day?
9 Is there anyone who makes you do things that you don't want to do?
10 How would you feel about making a speech in front of a lot of people?

4.6 Dialogue halves

Outline Students memorise one side of a dialogue and then try to find a partner whose lines fit with theirs

Focus Encouraging learners to fix spoken utterances into short-term memory, and raising awareness about typical spoken interaction patterns

Level Elementary plus

Time 20 minutes plus

Materials and preparation Prepare some four-line dialogues which focus on a particular language area and are set in a particular context. The examples in the boxes overleaf are for a pre-intermediate group, and focus on the use of the present perfect in the context of talking about shopping. Each student will need a half-dialogue as shown in the boxes overleaf. For each half-dialogue from Box 39, for example, you need to make sure you have the lines that go with it from Box 40. If there is an odd number of students, two of them will need to share one half-dialogue, and if there are more than 20 in the class you will need to double up on some of the dialogues.

Procedure

1 Give each student one of the half-dialogues (making sure that you also give out the matching halves).

2 Ask the student to remember exactly what it says on their piece of paper. When they have done this, they place the dialogue in their back pocket or somewhere where they can't see it.

3 Invite the students up on their feet. Encourage them to mingle around, saying their lines to different people until they find the person whose half-dialogue seems to fit best with their own one.

4 Those who finish quickly can help those who are still trying to find their partner. When everyone has finished, ask them to sit together in their new pairs. Tell them to decide on who the two people are in their dialogue, and what the situation is. Can they add two more lines onto the end?

5 Ask the students to perform their extended dialogues to the rest of the class.

Note

This activity is a good way of mixing up students and challenging them to work with people they might not normally work with.

Box 39

A: Where have you been? B: A: It's taken a long time. B:	A: Where have you been? B: A: Did you get anything nice? B:
A: Have you seen Emma? B: A: On her own? B:	A: Have you seen Emma? B: A: Who with? B:
A: Have you been shopping? B: A: Why not? B:	A: Have you been shopping? B: A: Well, you'd better hurry up. B:
A: Who's been shopping? B: A: Oh, great! I'm starving! B:	A: Who's been shopping? B: A: Did you get anything nice? B:
A: Have the shops closed yet? B: A: Do you want anything? B:	A: Have the shops closed yet? B: A: Have we got any milk? B:

Box 40

A: B: Shopping. A: B: I know. It was really busy.	A: B: Shopping. A: B: No, it was too expensive.
A: B: I think she's gone shopping. A: B: Yeah, I think so.	A: B: I think she's gone shopping. A: B: On her own, I think.
A: B: No, not yet. A: B: I've been cooking dinner.	A: B: No, not yet. A: B: I know. I'm going now.
A: B: I have. A: B: Will you help me unpack it?	A: B: I have. A: B: Just a new pair of jeans.
A: B: No, I don't think so. A: B: No, I've been already.	A: B: No, I don't think so. A: B: No. I've just used the last bit.

4.7 Line by line

Outline The students learn the lines of a dialogue by heart by covering it up and trying to remember the next line

Focus Fixing the lines of a dialogue into working memory

Level Any

Time 5 minutes plus

Materials and preparation A short dialogue (up to 15 lines) containing language which it would be useful for the students to focus on.

Procedure

1 Give out the dialogue. Ask the students to read it through a couple of times. Help out with any queries about meaning or pronunciation.
2 Now ask them to cover it up with a sheet of paper. They then slide the piece of paper down to reveal only the first line. Can they remember what the next line is? If they can't remember the complete line can they remember anything from it?
3 They then uncover the next line to compare it with what they guessed. How similar is it?
4 The students go through the dialogue several times in this way until they have learnt it by heart.
5 Ask them to perform the dialogue with a partner without looking at the text.

Extension

Later on in the lesson (or in a subsequent lesson) ask the students to try performing the dialogue again without looking at the text.

4.8 Prompts

Outline	Students use a prompt to help them learn the lines of a dialogue
Focus	Producing accurate language and fixing lines of a dialogue into short-term memory
Level	Any
Time	20 minutes plus
Materials and preparation	Choose a dialogue which does not contain too much new language for the level of your class, and which is not too long (up to about 25 turns). The example below is for an upper-intermediate group. Make enough copies so that each student has one. Alternatively, each group can be given a different dialogue to work with.

Procedure

1 Organise the students into groups of three and give each student a copy of the dialogue.
2 Give them a chance to read it through and to discuss and sort out any problems of comprehension. Provide dictionaries if they need them and make yourself available to help out with language issues too.

3 Ask them to agree on the situation of the dialogue. Who are the characters? What is the relationship between them? Where is the dialogue taking place?
4 When they have done this, ask them to decide on which learner will take on each of the two roles. Give the speakers some time (but not too long) to try to roughly remember the lines for their character.
5 One person in each group now looks at the text (the prompt) whilst the other two do not (the speakers). The speakers should try to say the lines for their character. If they can't remember what to say the prompt should help them by providing one or two words of the line to act as a clue. It is important, before intervening, that the prompt allows the speakers sufficient time to try to recall what they have to say. It will be useful to demonstrate this yourself first with a couple of students. Initially the prompt will need to supply a lot of clues but, as the speakers start to feel more comfortable with the lines, the prompt will be able to withdraw more and more.
6 When the speakers feel that they know their lines off by heart, ask them to swap around roles within their group.

Extension

Ask the groups to perform their memorised dialogues for each other or for the whole class.

Notes

This activity is very accuracy focused (for both the prompt and the speakers) and there will often be a lot of correction of what the speakers are saying. However, because the focus is on getting the lines right, rather than on the learners' own use of English, this form of correction is relatively unthreatening for the speaker.

Box 41

A: So you're going at last.
B: Seems like it.
A: Is that yes or no?
B: Unless you've got some other idea.
A: I've run out of ideas. Why? Do you have any other ideas?
B: If I had I suppose I wouldn't be going, would I?
A: I suppose not. Anyway, I've tried everything.
B: You've tried everything?
A: We've both tried everything, I suppose. I suppose there's no point in hanging on. No point in trying again. No point in going over the same old ground again and again and again. Best to give up, I suppose. Cut our losses. Go, go. Try with somebody else.
B: There's nobody else.
A: You'll find somebody else.
B: So will you.
A: I dare say. Not to worry about me.
B: We did agree it would be best.
A: I know we agreed. I'm saying go, go. Only . . .
B: Only what?
A: It's your decision.
B: My decision!
A: Just so long as you realise. It's your decision.
B: We both agreed.
A: We both agreed but it's your decision, it's still your decision. You're the one who's going.
B: One of us has to go.
A: And you're the one. You've made the decision to go. I haven't. I can't make decisions for you. Just so long as you realise.
B: Do you want me to go or not?

From the play *After Liverpool*, by James Saunders

5 Rehearsing and performing

All real-life language use is a form of performance. Indeed, the term *performance* is often used by linguists to describe what we *do* with language, as opposed to what we *know* about language (called *competence*). In another sense, too, we use language to *perform* ourselves – to make public our own unique identity. We do this by using a common language and making it our own. We take other people's words and we recycle them for our own situation-specific purposes. In this sense, language production is an endless process of borrowing, adapting, rehearsing and performing.

The activities in this section ask the learners to work with texts which have already been planned and constructed by others. In the same way that actors are generally not expected to write great works of literature whilst they are simultaneously performing on stage, the learners here, free from the pressure of having to create language in real time, are able to focus on other issues surrounding the dialogues. These issues may include different ways of pronouncing and interpreting the lines, as well as strategies for making what they say more interesting for the listeners. The learners are also provided with the opportunity to rehearse and practise the dialogues a number of times, each time increasing their familiarity with the content.

The first half of the activities (Chanted dialogue (5.1), Sounding like a gringo! (5.2), It's not what you say . . . (5.3), Students perform the listening material (5.4), Improvising into a scene (5.5), Shadowing actors (5.6) and Dialogues with movement (5.7) explore ways of challenging the students to address issues of pronunciation, such as intonation, weak forms, connected speech and speaking clearly, through presenting a variety of dialogues to each other.

Who's next? (5.8), Conducted dialogue (5.9) and Performance to writing (5.10) ask the students to process or reformulate what they have heard at the post-performance stage, and Reader's theatre (5.11), Direct speech (5.12), No way, José (5.13) and Let's have a drink (5.14) encourage a certain amount of manipulation of the text in order to make the dialogues ready for performance.

5.1 Chanted dialogue

Outline	Students practise a chant which takes the form of a dialogue
Focus	Raising awareness about elision and linking in phrases (*do you want to?* . . . and *I need to* . . . in the example below), and making these lexical chunks memorable for learners
Level	Beginner to pre-intermediate
Time	20–30 minutes
Materials and preparation	You will need a copy of the complete chant for each student, plus a cut up copy of the jumbled up sentences, as in the example below, for each pair.

Procedure

1 Discuss with students what things they might say to guests visiting their homes in their own countries (*make yourself at home*, *would you like a drink*, etc.). Put their ideas up on the board.

2 Give out questions such as the ones in Box 42 to students and ask them to discuss which ones would be said to a guest in their homes, and to put them into a logical order.

Box 42

Do you want to come in?

Do you want to take your coat off?

Do you want to sit down?

Do you want a cup of tea?

Do you want a piece of cake?

Do you want to watch TV?

Do you want to look around?

Do you want to see the garden?

3 Chant the text in Box 43, aiming for as natural a pronunciation model as possible. You may need to practise the rhythm beforehand. Ask the

students to compare their order with the order in which the sentences come up in the chant.

Box 43

Joanna and Anita

Joanna Cumin? Joanna Cumin?
Anita . . . Anita . . . Anita Gohome
Joanna Takyucotof? Joanna Takyukotof?
Anita . . . Anita . . . Anita Gohome
Joanna Sitdown? Joanna Sitdown?
Anita . . . Anita . . . Anita Gohome
Joanna Cuputea? Joanna Cuputea?
Anita . . . Anita . . . Anita Gohome
Joanna Pisucake? Joanna Pisucake?
Anita . . . Anita . . . Anita Gohome
Joanna Wachtivi? Joanna Wachtivi?
Anita . . . Anita . . . Anita Gohome
Joanna Lukaround? Joanna Lukaround?
Anita . . . Anita . . . Anita Gohome
Joanna Seethegarden? Joanna Seethegarden?
Anita . . . Anita . . . Anita Gohome!!!

4 Ask the students to listen to the chant again, this time paying particular attention to the way the words are pronounced and flow together. Ask them to write down in any way they like some of the chunks of language from the chant.
5 Give out the written version of the chant and draw their attention to the pronunciation of the sentences.
6 Experiment with saying the chant in different ways. Ask students to repeat each line after you, and then ask them to say the questions while you reply with the 'Anita' lines. Eventually you can get to the stage where one half of the class ask the questions and the other half reply.

Extension

Ask students to make their own 'Joanna' and 'Anita' dialogues. You could suggest scenarios for these, such as a lazy teenager who won't get out of bed and her mother (Joanna Havsumbreakfast and Anita Stayinbed).

Notes

This idea for this activity came to me via an Italian student who told me that she had misunderstood 'Do you want to . . .' for 'Joanna' when first arriving in Britain. The pronunciation is not exactly the same, but 'Joanna' is certainly closer to the way advanced or native speakers pronounce 'Do you want to' than a model which gives equal emphasis to each individual sound.

Box 44 below, shows an example of a chant which focuses on the relationship between the present perfect and the past simple tense. This one came out of a staffroom discussion with Pam Turton. For more examples of chants which practise particular linguistic features see the wide range of *Jazz Chants* books written by Carolyn Graham (1978). See also By name and by nature (6.1).

Box 44

Where have you been?
I've been to the zoo.
What did you do?
I saw a kangaroo.
Where have you been?
I've been to the shops.
What did you buy?
I bought some lamb chops.
Where have you been?
I've been to the station.
What did you do?
I got some information.
Where have you been?
I've been to six schools.
What did you do?
I broke all the rules.

5.2 Sounding like a gringo!

Outline Learners imitate the accents of various native speakers of English (British, American etc.) when using the mother tongue of the class, and then try to transfer this way of speaking to their own use of English

Focus	Raising awareness about specific pronunciation features, including voice quality of the language being taught
Level	Intermediate plus
Time	30 minutes
Materials and preparation	Write out a translation, into the mother tongue of your class, of an excerpt from a dialogue (or, if it is short enough, the entire dialogue) that the students have already listened to. Each student will need a copy of this, plus the transcript of the same excerpt in English. This activity is mainly aimed at monolingual groups (but see the variation below).

Procedure

1. After doing the listening exercises in the book in your usual way, give out copies of the translation of the dialogue.
2. Divide the learners into groups according to how many speakers there are. Ask the learners to practise the dialogue in the mother tongue, with each person taking a role, but to try to do it with a very strong Scottish, New Zealand, English or American etc. accent (whichever one they feel most comfortable imitating or is most appropriate to the context in which you are teaching).
3. Initiate a feedback session on what they've just done. It may be appropriate to get a confident group to do their version for the whole group. Discuss with everyone which particular sounds made what they were saying sound 'gringo'. What specifically did they have to do with their mouths?
4. Give out the English version of the dialogue. Ask them to do the conversation again, this time in English. Encourage them to try to transfer to the English version what they did with their mouths when sounding like a foreigner in the mother tongue.
5. Play the tape again at the end so that learners may internally assess how 'gringo-like' their own speech sounded. Ask them to discuss this in small groups.

Variation

With multilingual groups, give out the dialogue in English to mixed nationality groups of three. Two people should read the dialogue whilst the third listens to how they are saying the lines. The listener then gives the speakers feedback on how 'gringo-like' they sound and what features of their speech make them sound 'ungringo-like'.

Notes

This activity was inspired by 'Making Fun of English Sounds' in *Using the Mother Tongue* (2002) by Sheelagh Deller and Mario Rinvolucri. The word 'gringo' is widely used in Latin America, and to a lesser extent in Spain, as a mildly derogatory term for North American and British speakers of English. There may well be a more appropriate term to use in your own teaching context.

5.3 It's not what you say . . .

Outline	In pairs, students perform the same dialogue as others, but with different interpretations. They then try to work out what the other students' interpretations were
Focus	Raising awareness about the importance of intonation. Language development in the areas of interpretation and discussion of a scene
Level	Intermediate plus
Time	30–40 minutes
Materials and preparation	Choose or write a short dialogue which could be interpreted in different ways, and write out a list of different situations in which the dialogue could occur (see below). Each pair of students needs a copy of the dialogue and one of the interpretations.

Procedure

1 Arouse interest in the topic of the dialogue through discussion with the class. For the example below, for instance, you could ask questions like: 'Who normally asks people out, men or women?' 'At what age might it start happening?' 'Does this vary between different countries?' (for multilingual groups), 'Do you have any memories of asking someone out?' Depending on the dynamics of your group, this could be done either as a pairwork or whole group activity.

2 If you have the space, encourage students to get up so that they are able to move around freely. Give out a copy of the dialogue to each pair of students.

3 Ask them to practise saying it with their partner. Suggest that they try it as two people who don't know each other, and then as two people who do know each other. Encourage them to practise it until they don't need to look at the paper any more.

4 Discuss with the whole group what differences there were between the way they said the lines as strangers and when they knew each other.

5 Give each pair a different interpretation of the dialogue. With a large

group you can give out the same interpretation twice. Ask them to prepare to present their version to the rest of the class. They should add to the scene by including a few lines at the beginning or end of the dialogue which reveal more about the characters and situation they are portraying.

6 Students present their interpretations of the dialogue. Initially they should do this without the extra lines, and only using the dialogue they had been given. The other students discuss and comment on how they interpret what they have seen. The participants in the dialogue do not comment at this stage. They then present the dialogue again, this time with the initial lead in, and the class reassesses their initial interpretations.

Box 45

A: Do you fancy going to the cinema tonight?
B: Tonight?
A: If you're not doing anything else.
B: No, I'm not doing anything else.
A: Shall we go then?
B: Yeah, alright. If you like.

Interpretations

1 A is a very famous person. B is not a famous person and is very pleasantly surprised at being asked out in this way by someone who he or she has only just met.

2 A and B have been married for a very very long time. They never go to the cinema together any more. In fact they don't really do anything together any more.

3 A and B are teenagers at school. A has never asked anybody out before and B has never been asked out before.

4 A and B have been married for a very short time. B is having an affair and was planning to meet her lover tonight.

5 A and B have been happily married for ten years. It is their wedding anniversary today and B was hoping that they would be having a romantic candlelit dinner at home.

6 A and B both work in the same office. They are going out with each other but want to keep their relationship a secret from everyone else who they work with.

7 A and B are married. A few hours ago they had a huge row. This is the first time that they've spoken to each other since then.

Variation 1

Instead of giving out interpretations of the dialogues to different students, encourage them to decide themselves on situations in which the dialogue might occur. This will encourage more discussion between students at the planning stage, but may mean that you have less variety of types of dialogue at the presentation stage.

Variation 2

Instead of asking students to present their dialogues to the whole class, ask them to work with one other pair only. This will allow more student involvement and diminish the performance element for less confident students.

5.4 Students perform the listening material

Outline	Students perform the tapescript of the listening material from the coursebook, and their classmates answer questions about what they've heard
Focus	Challenging learners to use language which is above their current level in a way that others can understand. Raising awareness about differences between learners' interpretations of dialogues and more advanced speakers' versions of them
Level	Pre-intermediate plus
Time	20 minutes plus (depending on the number of dialogues used)
Materials and preparation	Find the tapescript of a series of short dialogues (typically found in the listening section of exams like PET (Part 1) and FCE (Parts 1 or 3), and cut it up into individual dialogues. You will need a different dialogue for each pair or group of three students, and also the recording of the dialogues.

Procedure

1 Distribute a different dialogue to each pair. Ask them to practise the lines until they feel comfortable saying them without looking at the text. If you have a third person in a group, ask them to act as director and prompt (see Prompts (4.8) in the previous chapter). Help out with pronunciation issues which arise as you monitor.

2 Tell the students to perform their dialogue to the rest of the class, and ask the students who are not speaking to try to answer the questions which go with that particular extract.

3 As each pair finishes, those who were listening give feedback to the performers on how clear their interpretation was, and whether they were able to answer the questions by listening to it.

4 Now play the original recording of the extract. What differences do they notice? Is this version easier or more difficult to understand? Ask the learners to redo the dialogue, having now heard the original recording and (if appropriate) trying to imitate the patterns used by the speakers.

5.5 Improvising into a scene

Outline	Students improvise a scenario that they have observed. They then work with the script of the same scenario, before finally seeing it performed by actors
Focus	Encouraging comprehension of a scene and activation of its language through use of a script
Level	Intermediate plus
Time	60 minutes
Materials and preparation	Choose a short scene of dramatic action from a film, a soap opera or a comedy programme where there are plenty of visual clues as to what people are saying. You will need the DVD excerpt and the transcript of exactly what was said. To save having to transcribe from the recording, try to get hold of the screenplay or script. Below is an example for an intermediate class using part of a *Fawlty Towers* episode.

Procedure

1 Discuss with the class what the characters involved in the scene are like and, if appropriate, what has happened previously.

2 Show them the scene with the sound turned down. As they watch, ask them to imagine what the people are saying.

3 In pairs (if there are two speakers in the scene), the students discuss what they think was being said. They then improvise the scene.

4 As they finish, give out copies of the transcript (see Box 46) and ask them to redo the scene with the script. Try to keep them on their feet, maintaining the authenticity and movement that was present at stage 3.

5 Show the scene on screen a second time, this time with the benefit of the sound.

Notes

Stages 4 and 5 are interchangeable. You may feel it is more appropriate to allow the class to first watch the scene with the sound before performing it, especially if you want the students to first notice particular aspects of pronunciation etc.

Variation

After giving out the script, ask the students to work together to practise pronunciation issues before they perform the complete dialogue, or after having watched the recorded version. If appropriate, they can also be asked to indicate word stress on the lines as they go through them, which they then compare with the recorded version.

Box 46

Basil Fawlty:	Good morning, madam, can I help you?
Mrs. Richards:	Are you the manager?
Basil Fawlty:	I am the owner, madam.
Mrs. Richards:	What?
Basil Fawlty:	I am the owner.
Mrs. Richards:	I want to speak to the manager.
Basil Fawlty:	I am the manager too.
Mrs. Richards:	What?
Basil Fawlty:	I am the manager as well.
Mrs. Richards:	Yes, I know, you've just told me; what's the matter with you? Now listen to me. I've booked a room with a bath. When I book a room with a bath, I expect to get a bath.
Basil Fawlty:	You've got a bath.
Mrs. Richards:	I'm not paying seven pounds twenty pence per night plus VAT for a room without a bath.
Basil Fawlty:	(*opening the bathroom door*) There is your bath.
Mrs. Richards:	You call that a bath? It's not big enough to drown a mouse. It's disgraceful.
Basil Fawlty:	(*muttering*) I wish you were a mouse; I'd show you.
Mrs. Richards:	*(standing next to the window)* And another thing: I asked for a room with a view.
Basil Fawlty:	(*to himself*) Deaf, mad, and blind.
	(*to Mrs. Richards as he makes a show of inspecting the view*)
Basil Fawlty:	This is the view as far as I can remember . . . Yes . . . Yes, this is it.
Mrs. Richards:	When I pay for a view, I expect to see something more interesting than that.
Basil Fawlty:	That is Torquay, madam.
Mrs. Richards:	Well, that's not good enough.
Basil Fawlty:	Well, might I ask what you expected to see out of a Torquay hotel bedroom window? Sydney Opera House, perhaps? The Hanging Gardens of Babylon? Herds of wildebeest sweeping majestically . . .

Mrs. Richards:	Don't be ridiculous. I expect to be able to see the sea.
Basil Fawlty:	You can see the sea. It's over there between the land and the sky.
Mrs. Richards:	I'd need a telescope to see that.
Basil Fawlty:	Well, might I suggest you move to a hotel closer to the sea. (*quietly*) Or preferably in it.
Mrs. Richards:	Now listen to me. I'm not satisfied, but I've decided to stay here. However, I shall expect a reduction.
Basil Fawlty:	Why? Because Krakatoa's not erupting at the moment?
Mrs. Richards:	No. Because the room is cold, the bath is too small, the view is invisible, and the radio doesn't work.
Basil Fawlty:	No, the radio works. You don't.
Mrs. Richards:	What?
Basil Fawlty:	I'll see if I can fix it, you scabby old bat.

From *The Complete Fawlty Towers*, by John Cleese and Connie Booth

5.6 Shadowing actors

Outline The class watch a scene and then gradually start imitating the lines used by the actors until they feel comfortable saying them on their own

Focus Encouraging natural reproduction of dialogic language in an appropriate context

Level Intermediate plus

Time 30 minutes plus

Materials and preparation Choose a short scene from a film or soap opera etc. where the actors speak reasonably slowly and the language is not too challenging for the students. You will need a copy of the transcript for each student, plus the clip (ideally on DVD, as this will allow you to do repeated showings more easily).

Procedure

1 Show the scene on the screen and discuss with the class what they understand about who the characters are and what they are talking about.

2 Give out the script of the scene and ask the class to read it silently as you play the scene again. Deal with any queries about meaning or pronunciation at this stage.

3 Now put the students into groups corresponding to the number of characters in the scene. Ask each student to start shadowing one of the characters. This will initially involve saying the lines to themselves as the

characters on the screen say them. The scene can be played several times and each time the volume is turned down slightly so that the voices of the students get increasingly louder and the actors' voices get increasingly quieter.

4 When you feel that they're ready, play the scene with the sound turned down completely, and ask them to read out the lines in their groups so that their performance is timed to what is happening on the screen.
5 Ask for a volunteer group to present their version to the rest of the class.
6 Now turn the recording off. Students perform the scene in their groups as it was done by the actors, incorporating any necessary actions.

5.7 Dialogues with movement

Outline	The class perform a simple dialogue whilst doing different actions suggested by the teacher
Focus	Building movement into dialogues to make their lines more memorable
Level	Elementary plus
Time	30 minutes
Materials and preparation	Each student will need a copy of a short dialogue suitable to their level. This could be focused around a particular area of language as in the elementary-level example in Box 47.

Procedure

1 Give out the dialogue to each pair of students. Ask them to practise it until they have learnt it off by heart.
2 Ask them to stand up and find some space (if you have some available).
3 Ask them to try out the dialogue again with you calling out some, or all, of the different ways of performing it from Box 48. You may need to mime some of the situations yourself if they're not sure about meaning.
4 Each pair now chooses one of the situations they have tried out and develops the dialogue by adding more lines either at the beginning or at the end. They should continue doing the actions they have chosen all the way through the complete dialogue.
5 Ask them to present their scenes to the others.

Note

Much of the dialogue that we enter into in non-classroom settings takes place while we are involved in other activities. Sometimes encouraging students to focus on action as well as words can help to make what they are saying more meaningful and memorable, and add a new level of interest each time it is performed.

Box 47

A: What are you doing on Saturday night?
B: Why?
A: Well, I'm inviting some people round and I need someone to help me cook.
B: Oh. I can't, I'm afraid. I'm going out.
A: Well, how about Sunday then?
B: Yeah OK. What time?
A: As early as you can. Is six o'clock OK?
B: No, not really. I won't be home until seven.

Box 48

a You're playing tennis
b You're working in the garden
c One of you is washing up and the other one is drying up
d One of you is cleaning the windows and the other one is reading the newspaper
e One of you is cleaning your shoes and the other one is cooking dinner
f You're dancing
g You're talking across a busy street
h One of you is driving and the other one is sitting behind
i One of you is pumping up the tyres on your bicycle and the other one is watching
j You're whispering because there's someone asleep in the same room
k You're watching a football match on television
l You're having dinner

5.8 Who's next?

Outline	Students work together to reconstruct a dialogue and then practise saying it in different ways
Focus	Encouraging students to notice language items used for invitations and suggestions. Challenging students to speak clearly
Level	Pre-intermediate plus
Time	20 minutes plus

Materials and preparation You will need enough copies of an invitations dialogue like the one below so that each student has one line from it.

Procedure

1 Organise the students into groups of between five and ten. If you have ten students in a group use all the sentences like the ones in Box 49. Otherwise take sentences off from the end of the conversation until you have the right amount. It is desirable to have students working in groups which are as close to ten in number as possible.

2 Give one strip of paper to each student in the group. Their task, as a group, is to work out the order of the conversation. They may not show their paper to anyone else and must decide on an order by saying their lines (several times if necessary) and discussing which one goes where. Do not intervene to help during this phase except where students are unclear about what to do. It is far better to allow the students to rely on their collective resources in order to complete the task. They will need to speak clearly and listen carefully to what others are saying, and negotiate within their group. With many groups operating at the same time, you may wish to set this up as a competitive race.

3 Once the group has agreed on an order you can get them to orally process the text in many different ways.

   a Ask them to run the conversation as quickly/slowly/loudly/quietly as possible.

   b Tell them to do alternate lines fast/slow or loud/quiet.

   c Tell them to start saying their line before the person before them has finished so that they are interrupting.

   d Challenge them to remember exactly what the person after them says (the last person will have to remember what the first person says). Ask them to rerun the conversation using what they remembered. This can be repeated many times.

   e See if they can run the whole conversation backwards.

4 Ask the students to try to recall all the ways in which suggestions were made in the text (*Shall we . . .*, *Let's . . .*, *How about . . .*, *Why don't you . . . ?*, *Couldn't we . . . ?*). Give them the written version of the complete conversation if they get stuck.

Extension

Ask the learners to work in threes and to produce their own dialogues using the structures which were extracted from the conversation.

Notes

This activity has its roots in the 'Teacherless Tasks' in *Towards the Creative Teaching of English* (1980) by Louis Spaventa and others, and later in *More Grammar Games* (1995) by Paul Davis and Mario Rinvolucri.

When you know a particular group of students it will be much easier to personalise the material for the jumbled up dialogue. For instance you could mention the names of the students, and include activities which you know they are interested in. The conversation could even be a reformulation of one that you overheard the students having. There is also no reason why the topic of the conversation should be limited to making suggestions.

Box 49

Shall we all go bowling tonight?

I can't. I've hurt my wrist. Let's go out for a meal instead.

Yeah, alright. Where, then?

How about Cafe Ikon?

It's a bit expensive. Why don't you all come round to my place and I'll cook something?

OK, but I don't know where you live.

Neither do I. Is it a long way?

We'd have to take a bus. Couldn't we meet here first and go together?

Alright. That's a good idea. Why don't we meet here at eight, then?

OK. Let's all make sure we're on time, then.

5.9 Conducted dialogue

Outline The students perform a dialogue as if each line is a different instrument in an orchestra

Focus Encouraging learners to focus on the way new language sounds

Level Any

Time 20 minutes

Materials and preparation	Prepare a short dialogue (or use one from the coursebook or other source) which is linguistically challenging for the learners and contains an appropriate quantity of new language items. The dialogue should consist of fewer lines than there are students in the class and should preferably not be longer than ten lines. Write out each line of the dialogue on separate pieces of card.

Procedure

1 Divide the class up into as many groups as there are lines and give each group a piece of card with a line on it.

2 Explain that you are going to conduct the students as if they were an orchestra. Whenever you gesture with your hand towards a group they should say their line. Demonstrate the gestures you will use to indicate different ways of saying the lines.

hand held down low: say the line with a low voice

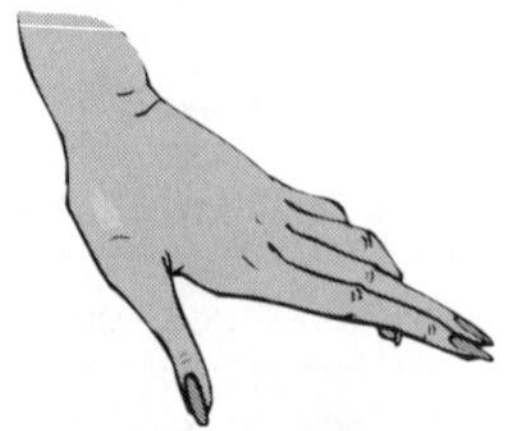

hand held up high: say the line with a high voice

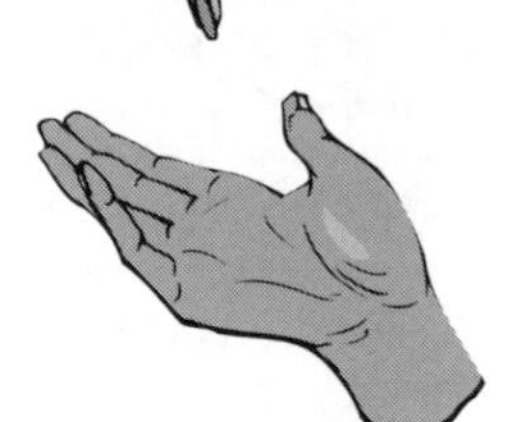

fingers stretched out wide: say the line very loudly

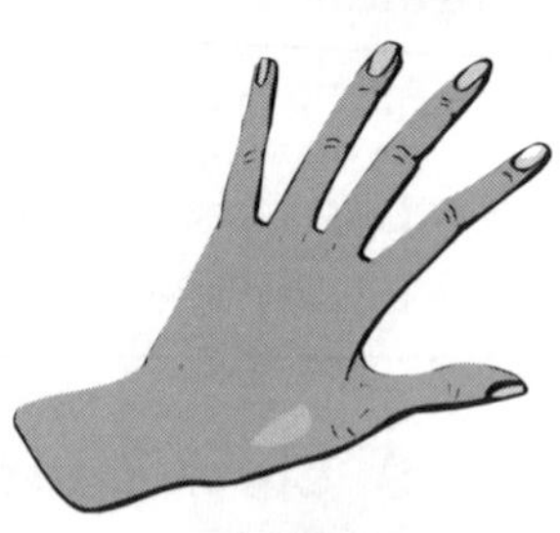

fingers held together: say the line very quietly

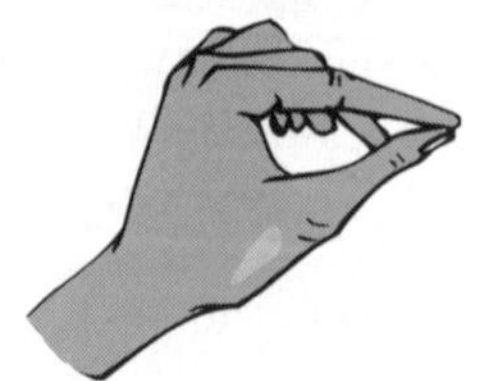

rotating hand: say the line repeatedly until you get the stop signal

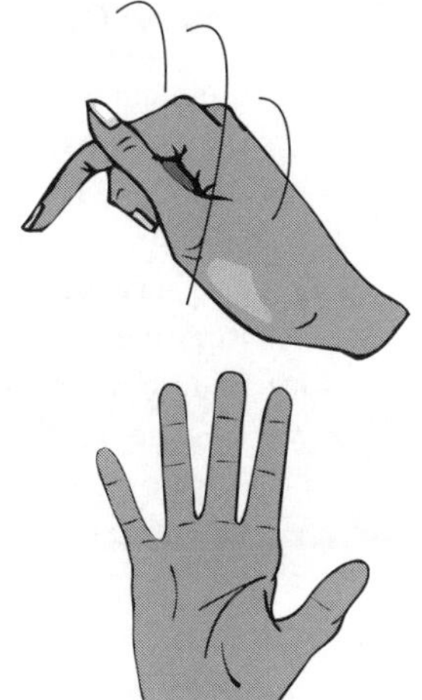

a policeman's stop signal: stop

3 Experiment with conducting the class. Try to use a variety of different ways of saying things. Do not focus on meaning, but on making an interesting 'piece of music'. Make no attempt at trying to put the utterances in the correct order. After this has gone on for a while, swap places with one of the students and get them to take on the role of conductor.
4 Ask the students to come up to the board with their pieces of card and leave them to organise them into the most appropriate order.
5 If you are using a dialogue which has a recording, play this to the students so they can check their answers against the recording.

Variation

Instead of complete utterances, give each individual/pair/group one word or chunk of a sentence only on a piece of card. This should include a grammatical or lexical area that you wish to focus on with the class. Conduct the students as above, and then ask them as a whole group to try to stick up all the words on the board to form a sentence with appropriate word order.

Note

This activity appeals to learners with musical learning styles because it provides a purely oral/aural way into the language focus. Sometimes learners in language classrooms are not expected to focus on the sounds of language until they have addressed issues of meaning. In the world outside the classroom however, sound may come before meaning. Learners may sometimes start noticing the way a word sounds before they are fully aware of its meaning, and this process may be an incentive to discover meaning.

5.10 Performance to writing

Outline	Students perform jokes to the rest of the class, who then produce a written version of what they have seen and heard
Aims	Encouraging students to orally activate written language. Developing speaking, listening and writing skills and raising awareness about the gap between the learners' own texts and more advanced versions
Level	Intermediate plus
Time	60 minutes plus
Materials and preparation	Choose some jokes which contain a mixture of narrative and dialogue (see Box 50 for some examples). Each pair, or group of three students, will need one joke.

Procedure

1 Organise the students into pairs or groups of three. Give each group one of the jokes you have selected. Help with comprehension where possible, but if no one in the group feels that the joke is funny it will be better to give them a different one. Ask them to prepare to present the joke as a performed piece to the rest of the class. They will need to think about how to stage it (if there is space available), and how the lines will be delivered. As they practise their scenes, monitor carefully and provide input where it is required. They should get to the stage where they can perform the joke without having to look at the text at all.

2 When everyone's ready, students perform their jokes in front of the class, whilst the others watch.

3 Now ask the class to review the jokes they watched by retelling them in their groups. Which one was the funniest?

4 Ask each group to work together to write a written version of the joke that they found the funniest. They should not, of course, write up their own one, but may refer to it for a model of style and the conventions which apply to jokes. You may wish to draw their attention to the use of a short, introductory, scene-setting lead in, the use of direct speech with appropriate punctuation, and the fact that jokes tend to be written in the present tense.

5 Give out the written copies of all the jokes so that the students can compare what they wrote with the originals. Are there any ways in which their versions could now be improved?

Box 50

Jokes

After having some medical tests, a man is asked to go back and see his doctor. 'I'm afraid I have some bad news and some worse news,' says the doctor.

'Oh dear, what's the bad news?' asks the man.

The doctor replies, 'You have only twenty-four hours to live.'

'That's terrible', says the patient. 'How can there possibly be worse news than that?'

'I've been trying to contact you since yesterday', the doctor replies.

A food expert is giving a talk to a large group of old people in a hospital.

'At your age you need to be very careful about what you eat. Lots of meat can be bad for your stomach, and too much sugar can mean that you put on a lot of weight. There is also one kind of food that can cause pain and suffering for years after eating it. Can anyone tell me what that is?'

An old man in the front row stands up. 'Is it wedding cake?' he asks.

A woman goes into a bar and orders twelve glasses of wine. She starts to drink them as quickly as she can.

'Why are you drinking so fast?' says the bartender.

The woman replies, 'You would be drinking just as fast if you had what I have.'

The bartender looks at her curiously and says, 'What do you have?'

The woman responds, 'An empty purse.'

A woman gets onto a bus with her baby. The bus driver says 'Wow! That's the ugliest baby I've ever seen. Ugh!'

The woman is shocked. She goes and sits down at the back of the bus. 'The bus driver was just really rude to me', she says, angrily, to the man sitting next to her.

'That's terrible', says the man. 'Go and complain to him. Go on – I'll hold your monkey while you do it.'

Two men are out walking in the countryside. Suddenly one of them collapses on the floor. The other is very worried and, taking his mobile phone, calls the emergency services.

'My friend is dead! What can I do?' he says.

'Take it easy. I can help', says the operator. 'First let's make sure he's dead'

There is a silence. Then a gunshot is heard. The man's voice comes back on the line. He says, 'OK, now what?'

Variation

Instead of each group having a different joke, this activity can also be done using only two jokes. Half the class work on one of the jokes, whilst the other half work on the other one. They then pair off with a group who have a different joke and perform to each other. Each group can now produce a written version of the joke that they have just seen. With large classes this variation allows for more student use of language in the same time span, and means that less confident students do not need to perform in front of the whole class.

5.11 Readers' theatre

Outline	Students perform a story as if it were a dialogue between them
Focus	Activating the language of a story and bringing it to life
Level	Pre-intermediate plus
Time	30 minutes plus
Materials and preparation	Choose a short story containing a mixture of narration and dialogue with plenty of action. Each student will need a copy of the written version of the story. See the examples below.

Procedure

1. Tell the class the story you have chosen to work with, using as much expression, gesture and mime as possible to help with comprehension.
2. Give out the written version of the story. Ask the students to work in pairs and to take turns reading it out loud to each other. Help them out with issues of meaning or pronunciation as they do this.
3. Tell them that they are going to perform the story together. They need to break it up into manageable chunks and share out the lines, so that the story bounces back and forth between them like a dialogue. For example:

   A: *A man was taking some straw to market on the back of his donkey.*
   B: *It was a hot summer's day and as they were going along the man started to feel very tired.*
   A: *He lay down by the side of the road and went to sleep . . .*

   As the students say their lines, the events of the story can be indicated with simple actions. For instance the first line above could be said whilst miming holding the reins of a donkey. The idea is to hint at the actions, rather than replicate them, so the scenes can actually be performed in quite limited space. It works best if the lines of dialogue for each character in the story are always read by the same person.

4 Encourage the students to practise the story until they are comfortable with it. For an extra challenge they can be asked to memorise their part.
5 Ask one or two pairs to perform their version of the story for the rest of the class.

Variation

Give different stories to different pairs. This way, students will be seeing stories that are new to them at the performance stage.

Notes

For more information about readers' theatre, including methods of scripting, staging and performing, see: www.aaronshep.com/rt.

The stories below were told to me by students at the Brasshouse Centre, Birmingham.

Box 51

The clever boy (a story from Iran)

A man was taking some straw to market on the back of his donkey. It was a hot summer's day and as they were going along the man started to feel very tired. He lay down by the side of the road and went to sleep. When he woke up he looked all around for his donkey but he couldn't see it anywhere. He saw a little boy standing by the side of the road.

'Have you seen my donkey?' he asked.

'A donkey carrying straw?' asked the boy.

'Yes', said the man.

'With a bad left leg?' asked the boy.

'Yes', said the man.

'And blind in its right eye?' asked the boy.

'Yes!' said the man. 'Where is it?'

'I haven't seen it', said the boy.

The man was furious and didn't believe the boy. He took him to the judge, accusing him of stealing his donkey.

'If you didn't steal the donkey', asked the judge 'how do you know so much about it?'

'Well', replied the boy, 'I saw that there were lots of bits of straw by the side of the road, so I guessed that the donkey had been carrying straw. Then I saw that the footprints on the right side of the road were deeper than those on the left, so I worked out that the donkey must have a bad left leg. Finally I saw that the grass had been eaten on the left side of the road but not at all on the right, so I assumed that the donkey must be blind in its right eye.'

The judge congratulated the boy on his intelligence and let him go free.

Box 52

Wars and Sawa (a story from Poland)

There was once a poor fisherman called Wars. One day when he was fishing in his boat on the river Vistula a terrible storm started. His boat was turned upside down and Wars fell into the river. He was a good swimmer but the storm got worse and worse and he started to swallow more and more water.

'Somebody help me!' he shouted but there didn't seem to be anyone around.

Eventually he started to sink down to the bottom and he was sure that he was going to die.

Suddenly he felt himself being lifted up. He turned to see a beautiful mermaid holding him in her arms. She carried him up to the surface and put him safely on the bank again. Wars looked into her eyes and immediately fell deeply in love with her. They kissed and suddenly the mermaid changed into a woman.

'Thank you', said Wars, 'you saved my life. What is your name?'

'My name is Sawa', said the woman, 'and thank you too. Your kiss has broken the spell which was put on me by an evil witch. She turned me into a mermaid and told me that the only thing that could save me was a kiss from a man who loved me. Now I am free.'

Wars and Sawa decided to spend the rest of their lives together. They got married and built a village on the banks of the river where they had rescued each other. That village still stands today and has grown into a huge city – the capital of Poland, Warsaw.

5.12 Direct speech

Outline	Students incorporate direct speech into a story and then perform it to a different learner
Focus	Providing practise in planning and performing direct speech when telling stories
Level	Intermediate plus
Time	30 minutes
Materials and preparation	You will need two short stories, urban myths or jokes which are written in a format which contains little or no direct speech, but where there is the possibility of incorporating more. See the two example urban myths in Boxes 53 and 54 for an intermediate class.

Procedure

1 Using a story that the class are already familiar with, tell them a very small part which incorporates interaction. Do this in two different ways:

one using direct speech and one using reported speech. You could also present these two versions on the board. For example:

. . . so Little Red Riding Hood told her grandmother what big eyes she had.

. . . so Little Red Riding Hood said to her grandmother, 'Wow! Grandmother! What big eyes you have!'

Discuss how the second version requires more 'performance' on the part of the speaker, and is probably more interesting to listen to since it encourages the listener to imagine the words actually being said.

2 Give each half of the class one of the stories. Ask them to read it in pairs and make sure that they understand what happens.
3 Tell them that they are going to retell the story to somebody who hasn't read it and, in order to make it more interesting, they are going to incorporate more direct speech into the telling. Ask them to think of and write down some specific things that the characters in the story could say. Help them out with ideas as you go round the class.
4 Ask them to rehearse in their pairs, so that the direct speech fits naturally into the story, and so that it is said in the way that the characters in the story would say it. They should eventually be able to tell the story in their own words without looking at the original.
5 Now, split the pairs up so that you have one student from one side of the class working with one student from the other. Ask them to share their new versions of the stories with each other.

Box 53

It was a dark and cold evening and an electrician was driving home after a long day at work. He saw a young woman hitchhiking by the side of the road. He was surprised to see her without a coat, and stopped to ask her where she wanted to go. She told him the address and, as he knew where it was, and it was so cold outside, he told her he could take her all the way to her house, but she would have to sit in the back of his van. She thanked him and got in. When they got to her house he stopped and got out to open the back of his van. To his amazement the girl had disappeared. He went and knocked on the door of the house and told the man who answered what had happened. The owner of the house was very shocked, and told him that the girl he described sounded like his daughter, but that she had been killed in a car accident exactly one year previously.

Box 54

Two young men were on holiday in Australia. They were driving along a quiet country road when suddenly their camper van seemed to hit something. They were worried and, when they got out to have a look, they saw a kangaroo lying dead in front of them. One of them suggested that it might be funny to dress the kangaroo up in some of their clothes. He put his sunglasses and jacket on the kangaroo and they started to take photographs of it. Suddenly the kangaroo jumped up. It wasn't dead at all – only stunned. It started to jump off into the desert. They knew they would have to catch the kangaroo because all of their money and credit cards were in the jacket pocket. Then they realised that they wouldn't be able to go after it in the van because the keys were also in the jacket pocket. They were horrified as they saw the kangaroo disappearing into the distance.

Note

Asking students to transform direct speech into reported speech has become a traditional classroom activity. However, if we want learners to develop the ability to tell stories in ways which are interesting for the listener, then being able to produce direct speech appropriately is also an important skill. As direct speech involves performing the actual words used, it can help to give the listener the feeling of actually being there.

5.13 No way José

Outline	The teacher dictates a range of expressions for agreeing and disagreeing. These are then used in mini dialogues by the students
Aims	To provide controlled practice of expressions for agreeing and disagreeing.
Level	Pre-intermediate plus
Time	30 mins
Materials and preparation	Prepare a transparency (or a handout) showing the discussion questions (Box 55) and some useful expressions for agreeing or disagreeing (Box 56). Each student will also need a worksheet like the one in Box 57.

Procedure

1 Ask the students to take a piece of paper and divide it into two equal columns, one entitled 'agreeing' and the other entitled 'disagreeing'. Randomly dictate the expressions and ask them to write them in what

they feel is the appropriate column. As you read, try to imagine a situation in which each might be used and say them as naturally as possible. They may encounter problems with meaning and spelling, but don't make things too easy for them by stressing what would normally be unstressed syllables. By saying the expressions as they would naturally be said, you will be encouraging them to focus on areas of pronunciation that they might otherwise have overlooked.

2 Ask them to work in threes on the discussion questions (Box 55).
3 Initiate a feedback session on the tasks and show them the transparency (or handout) so that they can check their spelling etc. Re-model the expressions as you go through them, again as naturally as possible. You may feel it's appropriate to drill them at this stage.
4 Hand out the A and B suggestion sheets (Box 57) to alternate students and ask them to make the suggestions to their partners who respond in any way they feel appropriate.
5 Ask them to develop some of their mini dialogues into longer conversations.

Box 55

Work with two other people to do the following tasks:

- Check your spellings with each other
- Put the phrases in order of strength
- Which expressions do you feel comfortable using? Why/Why not?

Box 56

Agreeing	**Disagreeing**
That's true.	You must be joking!
I agree.	I don't agree!
Yeah . . . I know.	I'm not so sure about that.
Yeah . . . you're right there.	Do you really think so?
Oh . . . definitely!	Rubbish!
Mmm, I suppose so.	

Box 57

Student A

Express the following opinions and suggestions to your partner and see how they respond.

This is a brilliant school, isn't it?
People are really cold here, aren't they?
The weather's getting better, isn't it?
We should all go out for a drink tonight?
It would be good to get married.
You remember you owe me £50?
The food's pretty bad here, isn't it?

Student B

Express the following opinions and suggestions to your partner and see how they respond.

We shouldn't have to pay to study English.
It's lovely weather here, isn't it?
It's a bit cold in here, isn't it?
Smoking should be banned, don't you think so?
Watching television's probably the best way of learning English.
This class is great.
You'll be able to help me move house tomorrow, yeah?

5.14 Let's have a drink

Outline	A student makes a suggestion to the class and the idea is responded to positively
Focus	Presenting and practising language for making suggestions and everyday activities
Level	Any
Time	5 minutes
Materials and preparation	None

Procedure

1. Invite the students to stand up, preferably where there is a little bit of space to move.
2. Give them a possible continuation for the sentence head *Let's . . .*, (e.g. *Let's have a drink*). The students then respond in unison with the reply, *Yes, let's have a drink*, before they all mime the action. Nominate a student to think of a different continuation, and the process continues until each student has had at least one turn at choosing a sentence.

Notes

Having the students repeat the speaker's sentence before miming it, not only serves the purpose of ironing out any language problems in an unthreatening way, but also builds their confidence by having their ideas reinforced by the whole group.

I first learnt this exercise from Jon Trevor in a games workshop at the Friends' Institute, Highgate, Birmingham.

Variation

At higher levels a greater range of language for making suggestions can be used (*Why don't we . . .*, *It'd be a good idea to . . .*, *I think we should . . .*, *How about . . .* etc.).

6 Co-constructing

Many learners give a higher value to being able to speak in a foreign language than being able to write in it. For this reason, speaking activities have become a prominent feature of many language learning courses. However, in terms of language development, writing has a certain advantage over speaking in that the writer is not normally under pressure to produce language quickly and in real time. Speakers need to maintain a reasonable pace so that they do not lose the attention of the person who is listening, and they therefore have little time available to attend to linguistic form. Writers, on the other hand, secure in the knowledge that their audience is not waiting impatiently for a message to be delivered, tend to be able to allocate more attention to accuracy, by, for example, consulting other learners, the teacher or dictionaries when needed.

The activities in this section focus on spoken language, but take a more analytical and reflective approach than is sometimes offered, asking the learners to plan, structure and perhaps modify the contents of the dialogues they produce. Although the dialogues which are constructed should ideally be meaningful and communicative, the principal aim with these activities is to produce dialogues which activate and contextualise particular areas of language.

This also has implications for the role of correction from the teacher and other learners. Reformulating or correcting learners' utterances whilst they are engaged in meaningful communication can sometimes have a detrimental effect on the communication itself. It may give the message that the form of the utterance is more important than its content. Correction at the planning or reflection stage however, because of the relative distance between the speaker and the words, and the fact that the learner is not simultaneously attempting to communicate, is far less inhibiting and probably more likely to be accepted and acted on by the learner.

The first section of this chapter looks at ways in which dialogues may be co-constructed through teacher input. By name and by nature (6.1) and Half a conversation (6.2), ask the learners to reactivate language originally used by the teacher into the dialogues they construct. In Dialogue building (6.3) and Community language learning (6.4), the teacher's role is to reformulate and improve upon dialogic utterances initiated by the learners themselves.

The last few activities, Writing dialogue articles (6.5), Famous last words (6.6), Dialogue into song (6.7), and Conversational involvement (6.8), ask the learners to incorporate particular lines into their dialogues, the idea being that this will challenge them to operate at a higher language level than they might do without this controlling feature.

6.1 By name and by nature

Outline	The teacher tells a story and the students reflect on what happened by scripting and performing a dialogue between the characters
Focus	Raising awareness about the use of weak forms and the way words run into one another in connected speech. See the example stories below for specific structures
Level	Any
Time	10 minutes plus (depending on the story used)
Materials and preparation	Choose a story to tell to the class, about two characters, in which there is a repetitive element (see examples below). The names of the characters should reflect the structures that they repeatedly use.

Box 58

a Mr Shuduv and Mrs Shuduntuv (Intermediate plus)

Mr Shuduv (the pronunciation is exactly the same as the weak form of *should have* as in *You should have told me*!) meets Mrs Shuduntuv (*shouldn't have*). Their eyes meet across the crowded bar and it's love at first sight, etc.

They get married and move to Chile and have two children, John and Mary. They use the Chilean system of adopting both parents' names in the surname, so the children are called John . . . Shuduv Shuduntuv and Mary . . . Shuduv Shuduntuv.

One day the family decide to drive to the mountains on holiday. They haven't got a car. Mrs Shuduntuv goes to a garage to buy a second hand one. She buys the first one she sees without checking it (£100,000).

They set off on holiday. The children start arguing in the back of the car. Mrs Shuduntuv is driving. She shouts at them. She tells her husband to give them a sandwich. Mr Shuduv says he didn't make any. The children start screaming for ice-cream. Mrs Shuduntuv tells Mr Shuduv to buy them one. He says he hasn't got any cash on him. The children start hitting each other. Mr Shuduv turns round to try to stop them. Mrs Shuduntuv tells him not to. She goes through a red light. The car hits a police car. The policeman makes them all get out of the car. Mrs Shuduntuv forgets to put the hand brake on. The car rolls over a cliff. The whole family walk back to their house. They try to open their front door. Mr Shuduv has forgotten the door key. They have to sleep in the garden.

Procedure

1 Tell the story to the class, drilling the names of the characters as you introduce them.
2 Working in pairs or small groups, the learners script a dialogue between the two characters and then rehearse and perform it.

Note

The technique of giving characters names which sound like the grammar being practised is a way of making the language focus more memorable for students.

Pictures, either drawn by the teacher or from a magazine will really help to set the context for the stories in Boxes 59 and 60.

Box 59

b Canavsum and Hiyuwa (Beginners plus)

Canavsum (*Can I have some . . . ?*) is a very lazy man (*show picture*). He is married to Hiyuwa (*Here you are*), a very helpful and hardworking woman (*show other picture*). Canavsum is always asking his wife to get him things: Can I have some cake?, Can I have some coffee etc. He never gets anything himself, and just watches television all day. Hiyuwa always gives him what he wants (*here you are*). Canavsum gets fatter and fatter and fatter, and Hiyuwa gets thinner and thinner and thinner.

Box 60

c Shwe and Istu (Beginners plus)

Shwe (*Shall we . . . ?*), a very happy looking woman, is married to Istu (*It's too . . .*) her unhappy looking husband (show pictures). Shwe loves life and is always wanting to do things (Shall we go to the beach?, Shall we go shopping etc.). Istu hates the world and never wants to do anything (It's too cold, It's too expensive etc.).

6.2 Half a conversation

Outline The students try to complete a telephone dialogue from the clues contained in what the other person says

Focus Appropriate responses in a dialogue

Level Pre-intermediate plus (see the variations on p. 140 for higher levels)

Time 30 minutes

Materials and preparation Choose or script a short telephone conversation where one person's lines can be predicted by what the other person says. Each student will need a copy of the dialogue with half the lines missing (see Dialogue B in Box 62 for an example) as well as a copy of the complete dialogue (Box 63).

Box 61

Dialogue A

A: Hello.
B:
A: Chris!! How are you?
B:
A: Oh, I love it. There's so much space.
B:
A: No! I haven't actually! It's freezing!
B:
A: The upstairs bathroom?
B:
A: OK, I'll go down and have a look in a minute. There's something else I wanted to ask you, actually.
B:
A: Well, there's some chicken in the fridge . . .
B:
A: No, it's alright. The sell by date is tomorrow.
B:
A: Well, I'm not really into spicy food, actually. Anyway I'm not much of a cook. Have you got any recipe books anywhere?
B:

Box 62

Dialogue B

A:
B: Hi. It's Chris.
A:
B: Fine, thanks. What do you think of the house?
A:
B: Yeah, it's too big for us really. I was going to say . . . have you worked out how to turn the heating on? I forgot to tell you.
A:
B: Oh, I'm sorry. There's a switch in the bathroom cupboard.
A:
B: No . . . the one downstairs. I've written a note and stuck it next to it.
A:
B: Yeah, what's that?
A:
B: Oh God, I forgot about that. It must have gone off.
A:
B: Ok, well eat it, then. You could make a nice curry out of it.
A:
B: Yeah, there are hundreds of them on the kitchen shelf. How did you manage to get to your age without being able to cook?

Procedure

1 Explain to the class what the situation of the dialogue is (in the example below somebody is staying at a friend's house and the friend, who is away, phones up). Tell them they are going to try out the dialogue as a telephone conversation. Elicit from them which topics might need to be discussed (with this example, topics may include: *how to turn things on, where things are, what needs to be done, and which things it's OK to use* etc.).
2 Ask them to work in pairs, to decide who will play each role, and to try out the conversation.
3 Speaking into a real phone or miming, perform Dialogue A (Box 61) to the class, leaving a suitable time gap for the missing response from B.
4 Ask the class to discuss in pairs which topics came up in the conversation.
5 Give out the dialogue containing the other person's utterances to the

students (Dialogue B). Ask them to work in pairs to decide on a suitable line for A for each gap. They will be working from memory, and from what they feel seems to fit with B's lines. Stress that it doesn't matter if what they write is not exactly the same as what you said, but it should make sense with the rest of the dialogue.

6 If they get really stuck ask them to turn over their sheets and then perform Dialogue A again for them. They then turn their sheets back over and write what they can remember now.
7 Give out the complete dialogue and ask them to compare it with what they wrote.

Box 63

Complete dialogue

A: Hello.
B: Hi. It's Chris.
A: Chris!! How are you?
B: Fine, thanks. What do you think of the house?
A: Oh, I love it. There's so much space.
B: Yes, it's too big for us really. I was going to say . . . have you worked out how to turn the heating on? I forgot to tell you.
A: No! I haven't actually! It's freezing!
B: Oh, I'm sorry. There's a switch in the bathroom cupboard.
A: The upstairs bathroom?
B: No . . . the one downstairs. I've written a note and stuck it next to it.
A: OK, I'll go down and have a look in a minute. There's something else I wanted to ask you, actually.
B: Yeah what's that?
A: Well, there's some chicken in the fridge . . .
B: Oh God, I forgot about that. It must have gone off.
A: No, it's alright. The sell by date's tomorrow.
B: Ok, well eat it, then. You could make a nice curry out of it.
A: Well, I'm not really into spicy food, actually. Anyway I'm not much of a cook. Have you got any recipe books anywhere?
B: Yeah, there are hundreds of them on the kitchen shelf. How did you manage to get to your age without being able to cook?

Variation 1

Photocopy Dialogue B onto a transparency for each pair and ask them to write up their complete dialogue on it. Some of these can then be evaluated with the whole class together (by using an overhead projector) before showing them the original complete dialogue.

Variation 2

With a higher level group, instead of doing stages 3–6, give out Dialogue A to half the class and Dialogue B to the other half. Ask them to decide on a suitable line for each of their gaps. This is more challenging since it requires that they work only from the clues given in the other person's lines. If they get stuck, one person from each group can be asked to perform their half of the telephone conversation for the others. When they've filled in as much as they can, they can then compare their completed dialogue with a pair from the other group.

Variation 3

(Also for higher level groups.) After stage 4 perform the dialogue to them again. This time ask them to make a note of the key words you use in your part of the conversation. They then pool the notes they make, in pairs or small groups, and try to reconstruct the complete dialogue from what they have written.

6.3 Dialogue building

Outline	The teacher elicits a dialogue from the students and uses it as a basis for language practice
Focus	Using the language of simple dialogues
Level	Beginner to intermediate
Time	20 minutes
Materials and preparation	None.

Procedure

1 Set the context of the dialogue, either by drawing some simple pictures on the board, or through mime and gesture. For instance a dialogue set in a restaurant could be suggested by drawing two simple stick figures, one sitting at a table and the other one standing (see p. 141). Adding a speech bubble from each figure will help to indicate that you want to work with what the people are saying.

2 Pointing to the waiter's speech bubble, elicit the first line of the dialogue from the students (*Are you ready to order?* for example). Write up one or two of the words from the line on the board as a prompt for the students to remember the line from (e.g. *order?*). Drill the complete utterance chorally and individually. Aim for natural ways of saying things.

3 Elicit the next line through gesture (or by drawing a fish on the board, for example), or accept an idea that one of the students comes up with. If necessary, you may need to reformulate what is elicited from the students to provide a more accurate version. You now have a two-line dialogue:

Are you ready to order?
Yes. I'd like fish and chips please.

Practise this by taking on one of the roles yourself, and choosing a student to take on the other one. Successive two-line exchanges can now be elicited, standardised, added and practised in the same way. Keep this process going until you have built up a dialogue of up to about twelve utterances, but which is represented on the board as a few words.

Dialogue	**On the board**
Are you ready to order?	*order?*
Yes. I'd like fish and chips please.	*fish*
Would you like salad or vegetables with that?	*salad or vegetables?*
What are the vegetables?	*vegetables?*
Peas and carrots.	*peas and . . .*
I'll have salad please.	*salad*

Anything to drink?	*drink?*
Have you got beer?	*beer?*
I'm sorry no. We've only got soft drinks.	*soft drinks*
OK, I'll have a coke please.	*cola*
With ice?	*ice?*
No, thanks.	*no*

4 Pointing at the prompts on the board, elicit the line that is represented by each one.
5 Now take on one of the roles yourself and perform the complete dialogue with a student taking the other role. Swap around so that you now do the other role with a different student.
6 Ask two students to practise the complete dialogue in open pairs, while the rest of the class listen. The whole class can now try out the dialogue in closed pairs.
7 Rub out the prompts on the board. Ask pairs to do the dialogue again without them.
8 Do the dialogue again with a student but this time introduce different food items.
9 Ask students to try out their own dialogues between a waiter and a customer, substituting their own food items.

Notes

This activity is particularly suited to focusing on the language of service encounters, either face to face or on the phone, (such as *shopping*, *booking a hotel*, *buying a ticket*, *ordering fast food*, *asking for information*, *checking in to a hotel or a flight* etc.), for interview type situations (e.g. *at the doctors*, *at customs*, *reporting an accident*, *friendly chat*, *friends meeting by chance*, *introductions*, *getting to know you* etc.), or as the context for functional language (*asking favours*, *inviting*, *giving advice*, *complimenting*, *apologising*, etc.)

With higher levels the teacher can be much less prescriptive about each utterance in the dialogue. The context of two people meeting for the first time at a party, for instance, is less predictable in terms of language, and a dialogue can be built which incorporates the ideas of the class much more. However, the teacher's role of reshaping the learners' utterances is still an important one.

6.4 Community language learning

Outline The class choose a topic to discuss and the teacher helps the learners express themselves by providing a reformulated version of their utterances (see also Talk and chalk (9.4))

Focus Creating a dialogue out of what the learners want to say

Level Any

Time 30 minutes plus

Materials and preparation For the recording stage you will need a hand-held dictaphone or other recording facility with a microphone on a lead. This activity is suitable for monolingual groups of up to 20 students, and (at beginners and elementary level) requires that the teacher has at least a working knowledge of the students' first language. See Variation 1 for working with multilingual classes and Variation 2 for larger groups.

Procedure

1 If the space available allows it, organise the class into a closed circle with you sitting on the outside. The recording equipment needs to be easily accessible for all learners.

2 Ask your students to have a conversation about a topic of their choosing. There are various ways of doing this. You could suggest that they start talking and see where the conversation goes, or you could give them a choice of different topics (for example, 'what we want to do in the future', 'planning an evening out', 'what happened last weekend' or 'how to get rich') and ask them to choose the one they prefer. If you want to direct them towards a particular area of language, you could specify the topic yourself.

3 If you're working with beginners, each learner says what they want to say in their mother tongue. You provide an English version of what they've said. They then practise the utterance in English until they feel comfortable with it, and then record it. Another student then has a turn, adding to what has been said, or answering a question posed by the previous speaker. Speakers are free to nominate the next speaker if they like (e.g. 'Alex, what did you do at the weekend?'). Or, as in real-life conversations, speakers can self-select.

4 In this way a recorded conversation is built up, line by line, with learners responding to what has been said before, or initiating new ideas, as they feel they want to. Students only need to record their utterances when they feel ready to do so.

The following conversation was recorded with a small group of Brazilian beginners. One member of the class (Alexsandro) has just left the group to go and work in the Amazon, and the others are discussing his journey.

Ricardo: *I wonder where Alexsandro is now.*
Julinho: *I don't know.*
Simone: *I don't know either.*
Luciandro: *Maybe he's in Rio.*
Camila: *I know that he is near Curitiba.*
Julinho: *Perhaps he's flying now.*
Simone: *Did he go by plane, Ricardo?*
Ricardo: *Luciandro told me before that he went to Rio, by bus.*
Julinho: *I don't understand. He's going by bus to Rio, and after . . .?*
Ricardo: *I don't know but maybe Camila knows or Luciandro.*
Julinho: *We don't understand. I thought he was going by plane.*
Luciandro: *Because he is going from Rio by plane. In a military plane.*
Julinho: *Thanks, I understand now.*

5 When it reaches an appropriate place (the conversation should not be too long) stop the recording and play it back to the learners. After each utterance, ask them to repeat what was said and to translate it back into the mother tongue. Write up each line on the board in dialogue format (see above) as you go.
6 You now have a useful resource which can be used for language analysis and practice. Learners are invited to ask you any questions they wish to about the language used in the transcript. With beginners this can happen in the first language of the class. They can be asked to practise the complete conversation in groups, before going on to develop different conversations around a similar theme ('I wonder where my brother is now . . .' etc.)

Notes

This process works better if it's not used as a one-off lesson. After initial awkwardness about the recording process, and the fact that the responsibility lies with the learners to initiate language, classes quickly get used to this way of working, and it can become a regular way of introducing a focus on language. Where a number of recordings are made over a longer period, the class can be given their own copies of the transcripts and the recordings, to keep as a record of the conversations they have had.

Community Language Learning was developed by Charles Curran in the 1970's and has been written about extensively by Earl Stevick and others. For more detailed examples of its application, see Stevick's *Teaching Languages: A Way and Ways* (1980) and, in this series, *Dictation* (1988) by Paul Davis and Mario Rinvolucri.

Variation 1

With multilngual classes, and at higher levels, it will not be possible or necessary for the teacher to provide translations of the learners' utterances. In this case the students can speak in English and the teacher can reformulate what they've said to provide a more accurate or more effective version. Some learners, however, will feel more comfortable recording straight away without the teacher reformulation stage. When this occurs, the reformulation can happen later at the transcribing stage.

Variation 2

For larger classes, and at post-beginner level, the learners can be asked to do the transcribing, rather than the teacher. In this case only some of the learners take part in the conversation building stage, and the rest of the class are kept actively involved by transcribing each utterance in their notebooks as you go along. At the end of the conversation they can then work together to write up their best version of it on the board, which is then compared with the recording.

Variation 3

Ask two students to sit at the front of the class. Ask them to co-construct the dialogue for a specific situation, using their own ideas or based on suggestions that are volunteered by the rest of the class. Again, the conversation is recorded line by line, but only when everyone is satisfied. Here the teacher can take a (literally) back-seat role, and suggest changes or corrections only at the stage when the dialogue is being played back.

6.5 Writing dialogue articles

Outline	Students write a dialogue-style article, based on an interview with their partner, where the partner has chosen the questions to be asked. This activity works well as a follow up to Working with interviews (1.11)
Focus	Encouraging personalised speaking and writing
Level	Elementary plus (the questions in Box 64 are aimed at pre-intermediate-level plus students)

Time	60 minutes
Materials and preparation	Each student will need a copy of a question sheet like the one below.

Procedure

1 Give out the list of questions to each student. Ask them all to choose seven questions that they could give interesting answers to, and would feel comfortable talking about. They should make the choice on their own, but help them out with language or provide dictionaries if they need them. Allow sufficient time so that they're not rushed into just picking the ones that they understand immediately.

Box 64

Question sheet

1 Where in the world would you most like to live and why?
2 What has been your most embarrassing moment?
3 Who in the world do you get on with the best and why?
4 What's your biggest regret?
5 What keeps you awake at night?
6 What are you most afraid of?
7 Which living person do you most admire?
8 Which living person do you most despise?
9 What makes you special?
10 What is your favourite journey?
11 What single thing would improve the quality of your life?
12 What is your favourite book?
13 What is the most important lesson life has taught you?
14 How do you relax?
15 Do you believe in life after death?
16 What is your most unappealing habit?
17 What is your idea of perfect happiness?
18 How would you like to be remembered?
19 How do you see yourself in ten years' time?
20 What's the craziest thing you've ever done?

2 Pair the students up. Now ask each student to interview their partner by asking the questions that have been chosen. The student who is interviewing makes notes as they go along.
3 When they've had a chance to swap round so that they've both been interviewed, ask them to convert their notes into a dialogue article. They will first need to decide on the most logical way of ordering the questions.
4 Display the dialogue articles around the room for other students to see and comment on.

Variation

If students don't write their names in the article, when the others read them they could try to work out who was interviewed.

Note

I learnt the idea of students choosing which questions they wanted to be asked from *Once Upon a Time* (John Morgan and Mario Rinvolucri, 1983).

6.6 Famous last words

Outline	Students write dialogues which develop towards a particular last line
Focus	Raising awareness about the context in which utterances fit
Level	Intermediate plus
Time	30–40 minutes
Materials and preparation	Each pair of students will need one of the utterances like those in the 'Last lines' in Box 65.

Procedure

1 Show students one of the 'last lines'. Elicit who might say it and in what sort of situation. By eliciting ideas from the whole class, build up a short dialogue on the board which ends with the line. For example:

A: *You know that alarm clock you lent me?*
B: *Yes.*
A: *Well, I'm really sorry but it doesn't seem to work any more.*
B: *You're joking! I've only had it a few weeks.*
A: ***I'll get you a new one. OK?***

2 Now give one 'last line' to each pair of students.
3 Ask them to discuss what could have been said before to lead to this line. They then construct a short dialogue (five to seven lines), which will

conclude with the line they've been given. They mustn't however, write the 'last line' on the sheet.

4 When they have finished, display the dialogues on the walls around the room, and redistribute the 'last lines' so that each pair has got a different one from before.

5 Their task now is to read the dialogues and stick the 'last line' at the end of the dialogue that they think it goes best with.

6 The original authors of the dialogues can now check whether their dialogues make sense with the last lines that have been added.

Box 65

Last lines

That's what I've been trying to tell you.
Look. I don't know. OK.
Wow! That was lucky!
Don't worry about it.
I just wish you could've told me.
I'll get you a new one. OK?
He always says that.
Is that it?
Well, it was nice to see you anyway.
Alright. That sounds like a good idea.
Well, if you're sure it's alright.
Of course you can!
Well, I don't think it is.
Well, whose is it then?
So am I. Let's go.
OK, well we can sort it out tomorrow.

6.7 Dialogue into song

Outline Students use the words of a song as a starting point for dialogue and then listen to the song to notice the order in which the words are used

Focus Helping learners understand the words of a song through having first performed its lines in a dialogue. Raising awareness about how pronunciation affects meaning

Level Intermediate plus

Time 60 minutes plus

Materials and preparation Find a song, the lyrics of which contain dialogue (an example for an intermediate class is given in Box 66). Split the dialogue up into bite-size chunks. Each student will need one of the chunks of dialogue.

Procedure

1 Discuss the themes of the song with the class. With the example below this might involve talking about conflict situations between parents and their children, or when is the best time to leave home.

2 Write up on the board a very short exchange which summarises the dialogue contained in the song. For instance:

Son/ Daughter : ( ) I'm leaving home.
Father/Mother: ( ) You can't.

Elicit ways in which the lines could be said. Put the students' ideas up in the gap as they say them. They could come up with anything from 'nervously' to 'looking for a fight'. Discuss with the whole class under which circumstances each manner of speaking would be used.

3 Put the students into pairs and get them to try out the dialogue in as many different ways as possible.

4 Give out lines of song dialogue (don't tell them it's a song yet) to groups of two or three. Ask them to discuss ways in which the lines could be said. They now work out a logical order for the lines and develop a mini scene which incorporates them.

5 Ask the groups to show their mini scenes, either to the rest of the class or to a different group. Those who are watching provide feedback on how they feel the lines were said.

6 Ask the students to stand up and come to the front of the class. Tell them one side of the room represents the beginning of the conversation and the other side the end. Play the song (there will be a stir when they realise the lines are part of a song) and ask the students to organise themselves in a line according to the order of the lines of dialogue. If you have more students in the class than the number of lines, and have consequently doubled up on some of the chunks, there will have to be some students joining the line together at the same point.

Extension

In small groups, ask the students to develop their own scenes around the themes which have been explored. With the 'Father and Son' example (see Box 66) these could include the last day at work, leaving your family to go and study in England etc. Ask them to perform these scenes to the rest of the class.

Box 66

'**Father and Son**' by Cat Stevens

Father/Mother: It's not time to make a change. Just relax, take it easy. You're still young that's your fault. There's so much you have to know.

Father/Mother: Find a girl, settle down. If you want you can marry. Look at me – I am old but I'm happy.

Father/Mother: I was once like you are now, and I know that it's not easy to be calm when you've found something going on.

Father/Mother: Take your time, think a lot. Think of everything you've got. For you will still be here tomorrow but your dreams may not.

Daughter/Son: How can I try to explain? When I do you turn away again. It's always been the same – the same old story.

Daughter/Son: From the moment I could talk I was ordered to listen. Now there's a way and I know that I have to go away.

Father/Mother: It's not time to make a change. Just relax, take it easy. You're still young, that's your fault. There's so much you have to go through.

Father/Mother: Find a girl, settle down. If you want you can marry. Look at me – I am old but I'm happy.

Daughter/Son: All the times that I've cried, keeping all the things I knew inside. It's hard but it's harder to ignore it.

Daughter/Son: If you were right I'd agree but it's YOU you know, not me. Now there's a way and I know that I have to go away.

Notes

Depending on the age of your students you may prefer to use the more recent Boyzone interpretation of 'Father and Son'. Other possible songs to use include 'America' (Simon and Garfunkel) and 'Space Odyssey' (David Bowie), but it is really worth finding a song which suits the interests of your students. Songs where the language is less dialogic but still resembles spoken language may also be used. For instance from the song 'Famous Blue Raincoat' by Leonard Cohen each pair of students can be given one of the lines from Box 67 below and asked to develop a telephone conversation between old friends. The line that they have been given should be used at some point in the conversation. The performing and listening stages then take place as described above.

Box 67

It's four in the morning
She said that you gave it to her
Thanks, for the trouble you took
What can I possibly say?
I miss you
the end of December
the last time we saw you
all through the evening
I hear that you're . . .
I like where I'm living

6.8 Conversational involvement

Outline	Students construct dialogues to illustrate the meanings of particular catchphrases
Focus	Understanding the meanings and uses of catchphrases and raising awareness about conversational involvement
Level	Upper-intermediate plus
Time	20 minutes plus
Materials and preparation	Each student will need a copy of dialogues like the ones in Box 68, and each pair will need a catchphrase like the ones in Box 69. Students will also need access to dictionaries.

Procedure

1 Give out the dialogues to the class and make sure dictionaries are available. Ask the students to complete each dialogue using the appropriate ending to each catchphrase. (Answers: 1 = Do as the Romans do. 2 = The merrier. 3 = Makes Jack a dull boy. 4 = The mice will play.)
2 Give each pair of students a catchphrase like the ones in Box 69. Ask them to construct a short dialogue which incorporates the catchphrase and illustrates its meaning, as in the examples. Again, they will probably need to consult dictionaries.
3 Ask the learners to perform their dialogues to each other.

Box 68

1

A: I see you've taken to wearing shorts.
B: Yes, well, as they say, when in Rome . . .
A: ______________________________
B: Exactly.

2

A: How many people are coming to the wedding?
B: I've lost count. But, as they say, the more . . .
A: ______________________________
B: Exactly.

3

A: I see you've taken up golf.
B: Yes, well, you know what they say: all work and no play
A: ______________________________
B: Exactly.

4

A: You're going away and leaving Babs on her own?
B: Yes, I'm a bit worried. Like they say, when the cat's away
A: ______________________________
B: Exactly.

Box 69

An apple a day keeps the doctor away.
Better the devil you know than the devil you don't.
Cleanliness is next to godliness.
Don't count your chickens before they are hatched.
Early to bed and early to rise makes a man healthy and wealthy and wise.
If a job's worth doing, it's worth doing well.
It's no use crying over spilt milk.
The grass is always greener on the other side of the fence.
There's more than one way to skin a cat.
Too many cooks spoil the broth.
Two wrongs don't make a right.
Absence makes the heart grow fonder.
The early bird catches the worm.
A bird in the hand is worth two in the bush.
Mighty oaks from little acorns grow.

Notes

The completion of B's utterance by A, as in the dialogues above, is a common feature of spoken language, and is a way of showing conversational involvement. Used sparingly, it indicates to the speaker that she is being listened to, and creates dialogue which is jointly, rather than solely constructed. When completion is overused however, it can be frustrating for the speaker, and it may be useful to discuss with learners how comfortable they feel about doing it, and in which situations they feel it is appropriate.

Variation

Give the learners copies of the dialogue in Box 70 (an extreme example of conversational involvement from *Monty Python's Flying Circus*). Ask them to practise saying it in pairs. Now give them different situations (for example a shop, a police station, a tourist information office etc.) and ask them to construct their own dialogues where one person's utterances are constantly being completed by the other speaker.

Box 70

Mr Vernon:	Hello, madam . . . (*comes in*)
Mrs Long Name:	Ah hello . . . you must have come about . . .
Mr Vernon:	Finishing the sentences, yes.
Mrs Long Name:	Oh . . . well . . . perhaps you'd like to . . .
Mr Vernon:	Come through this way . . . certainly . . . (*they go through into the sitting room*) Oh, nice place you've got here.
Mrs Long Name:	Yes . . . well . . . er . . . we . . .
Mr Vernon:	Like it?
Mrs Long Name:	Yes . . . yes we certainly . . .
Mr Vernon:	Do . . . Good! Now then . . . when did you first start . . .
Mrs Long Name:	. . . finding it difficult to . . .
Mr Vernon:	Finish sentences . . . yes.
Mrs Long Name:	Well it's not me, it's my . . .
Mr Vernon:	Husband?
Mrs Long Name:	Yes. He . . .
Mr Vernon:	Never lets you finish what you've started.

From Monty Python's *Flying Circus*

7 Creating and personalising

As in the previous chapter, the activities in this section encourage the learners to plan and script dialogues through working from some form of stimulus. Here, however, the learners are given more freedom in terms of the content and the direction of the discourse they develop. When learners centre the dialogues on topics which they themselves choose, and when they construct them along lines that they themselves decide, the dialogue is likely to be both more meaningful and memorable. More memorable, too, will be the individual words and phrases that they insert into their dialogues.

When learners work in pairs or small groups to create a dialogue there is a useful balance of controlled versus less controlled language use. There is a measure of control which is motivated by the need to jointly produce a final product that is both accurate and appropriate. Explicit peer teaching is often a feature of this type of activity, and learners can also simply 'pick up' a lot of language from those they are collaborating with.

At the same time, learners bring their existing language skills and knowledge to the process and there is a freedom to draw on all of this in order to create the most appropriate dialogue. There should also ideally be a certain amount of debate and free discussion as learners try to agree on the context in which the dialogue will occur, and the relative merits of including particular language items.

But simply asking learners to write a dialogue, without any overall structure or purpose, seldom works well. The task is too broad and unfocused. The activities included here, therefore, all use some form of stimulus in order to generate ideas. In What did we have to say? (7.1), The words I'd like to own (7.2) and Dice dialogues (7.3), language itself is the starting point for determining the course of the dialogue, and in Speech bubbles (7.4), Picture dialogues (7.5) and Dark secret scenes (7.6), learners write dialogues based on their interpretations of pictures.

Soundtracks (7.7), Conscience alley (7.8) and From depiction to dialogue (7.9), all use physical action as a way of making the dialogues more meaningful, and in Semi-planned roleplay (7.10), The room talks back (7.11) and Into the future (7.12), it is the lives of the learners themselves which shape how the dialogues will develop.

7.1 What did we have to say?

Outline	Students plan and perform a dialogue incorporating particular language items
Focus	Providing a personalised context in which to activate language that has been previously focused on
Level	Pre-intermediate plus
Time	20 minutes plus
Materials and preparation	Choose some language items that have recently been focused on in class, write them out on small slips of paper and place them in a container of some sort. It is good if these include a mixture of single words (e.g. *reckon*) and lexical chunks (e.g. *at the end of the day*).

Procedure

1 Demonstrate the activity by taking out two slips yourself. Tell the class what they say and elicit suggestions for a conversation which could incorporate both language items. Discuss who the speakers are, where they are and what they are talking about.

2 Ask each pair of students to pick out two slips of paper and not to show their papers to anyone else.

3 Encourage them to discuss conversations that they could have where these two language items could naturally occur.

4 Students try out their conversations. They should aim for a dialogue of about 10–12 lines. Some pairs will finish before others. As they do so, allow them to pick another slip. Can they incorporate this new language item naturally into their conversation, or do they need to create another one?

5 Students present their conversations to the other students as naturally as possible. Those students who are watching try to work out which language items they were asked to incorporate.

Variation 1

Instead of keeping the dialogue in their heads ask the students to write it out.

Variation 2

With a more confident group, instead of allowing students to choose their own situations, ask the other learners to decide on the characters and setting for each of the improvisations. Students then have to spontaneously develop a scene and incorporate the language items as smoothly as possible.

Variation 3

Instead of picking language items to include in their scenes, students pick two words from a collection of adjectives of character. They then have to devise and then perform a scene where the two speakers exhibit these characteristics. The other students have to guess what characteristics were picked.

7.2 The words I'd like to own

Outline	Students pick out words from a tapescript in a coursebook and then produce a dialogue incorporating as many of them as possible
Focus	Encouraging learners to activate language items that they feel are important to them
Level	Pre-intermediate plus
Time	30 minutes plus
Materials and preparation	Each student will need a copy of the tapescript for the listening material you will be working with.

Procedure

1. After having done the listening exercises in the coursebook in whatever way seems appropriate for your class, give out copies of the tapescript.
2. Tell the students to underline words, chunks or even whole sentences that they'd like to 'own' (i.e. be able to use themselves as part of their active language).
3. In pairs ask them to compare what they've underlined, and to agree on one or two pieces of language to work with.
4. Ask each pair to write out a short dialogue of 5–10 lines which incorporates the language they have chosen to focus on. Monitor as they do this and check that the language point is being used accurately.
5. Students perform their dialogues to the rest of the class, whose task is to identify the piece of language they were practising.

Variation 1

Instead of using language from tapescripts, ask students (for homework) to pick out language they come across when eavesdropping on advanced or native speakers, or listening to English songs, films or soap operas etc. They then write a dialogue to include the language they heard.

Variation 2

Instead of asking students to perform their dialogues, ask them to display them around the room. Everyone then reads everyone else's dialogue and makes a note of the language items they think the dialogue is practising. This can then be checked with the authors.

7.3 Dice dialogues

Outline	Students construct a dialogue in which what they say is determined by the throw of a dice
Focus	Encouraging learners to think carefully about possible utterances in dialogues
Level	Elementary plus
Time	30 minutes
Materials and preparation	You will need a dice for each pair and some transparencies (if available).

Procedure

1 Give a dice to each pair of students.

2 Tell them they have to produce a short eight-line written dialogue where the number of words in each utterance will be determined by the throw of dice. For example, if A throws a '6' then the line that they write down for A must consist of exactly six words (contractions count as one word). Ask them to write up their dialogue on a transparency, and to include the number that was thrown at the end of each line. If you don't have an overhead projector available, then students could display their dialogues around the room instead.

3 Give them the topic for the dialogue. A good subject for this activity is 'arranging an evening out', as shown below:

1	A:	*Do you want to go out?*	(A threw a '6')
2	B:	*No.*	(B threw a '1')
3	A:	*Why's that then?*	(A threw a '3' (contractions count as one word))
4	B:	*Too tired.*	(B threw a '2')
5	A:	*How about tomorrow night then?*	(A threw a '5')
6	B:	*Where could we go?*	(B threw a '4')
7	A:	*Shall we go to the theatre?*	(A threw a '6')
8	B:	*OK. Where's the paper?*	(B threw a '4')

4 Display each pair's dialogue on the overhead projector. Do some whole group analysis of the texts. Areas to focus on may include, for example, speaking very directly (line 2 above), use of contractions (line 3), use of *then* (lines 3 and 5), ellipsis (line 4) and use of articles (lines 7 and 8).

With a competitive group you may wish to award points for each line that both complies with the dice throw and is error free.

7.4 Speech bubbles

Outline	Students fill in the empty speech bubbles of a comic strip story. They then tell their complete story to a different pair
Focus	Creating a motivating context in which to activate the dialogue contained in a story
Level	Pre-intermediate plus
Time	45 minutes
Materials and preparation	Each student will need a copy of a picture story like the one below.

Procedure

1. Give each pair a copy of the picture story.
2. Ask them to work in pairs and to discuss what they think is happening in each box and what is being said. When they have done this they write a line for each of the speech bubbles.
3. Ask them to practise telling the story in their pairs, incorporating the lines of dialogue.

Variation

With some stories (like the example above) it may be possible to split the story into two parts. Give half the class the first part of the story, and the other half the second part. Each half work together in pairs to complete the speech bubbles for their own half of the story. After practising telling it in pairs, each student now joins with someone from the other half of the class and retells the part of the story that they have worked with.

7.5 Picture dialogues

Outline	Students write a dialogue to go with a film still, and then try to find the dialogues which go with their classmates' pictures
Focus	Encouraging learners to explore possible dialogues for particular contexts. Extensive reading skills
Level	Elementary plus
Time	30 minutes plus

Materials and preparation You will need a collection of pictures showing people involved in a variety of different situations, displaying a variety of different emotions. Film stills are ideal for this (see for example www.home.comcast.net/~silentfilm/alphar.htm) but you could also use pictures from magazines or your own personal photos.

Procedure

1 Each pair of students is given one picture. They discuss what they think the people might be about to say, or might have just said. Then, on a separate sheet of paper, they write up their best ideas into a short dialogue.
2 Now collect the dialogues and pin them up around the room. Redistribute the pictures so that each pair now has a new one. They should not know who wrote the dialogue for this picture. Ask them to go round the classroom, reading each dialogue and trying to find the one which best fits their picture. Suggest that they read everything before making a decision. When they have found it, they pin up the picture next to the dialogue.
3 As a way of providing feedback, ask each pair to give a mini presentation to the rest of the class about their picture, what their dialogue is, and what prompted them to write it.

Variation 1

Use a range of stills from the same film, and ask students to create dialogues for them. This can be used as a way of generating interest in the film or, if it's a film that the class have already seen, as a way of reviewing it.

Variation 2

Instead of displaying the dialogues around the room, put the pictures up instead. Pairs now take turns to read or perform their dialogues while the rest of the class listen and decide which picture it represents.

7.6 Dark secret scenes

Outline Students improvise scenes from a soap opera about characters that they have created, and then convert these scenes into a written dialogue

Focus The language needed to create a dialogue which has emerged through improvisation

Level Pre-intermediate plus

Time	60 minutes plus
Materials and preparation	Two large pictures of people – they could be two characters in a soap opera. Students will find this activity easier if they have already done activities which examine the format of soap opera style dialogues (see for example Stage directions (2.4)).

Procedure

1 Show the class the pictures you have of the characters for the soap opera. Through asking questions, start to elicit their ideas about what kind of people they are. For example, you might ask:

What's her name?
How old is she?
What's her job?
What's she like?
Is she happy?
What does she like doing?
What annoys her?
What's her relationship to X?

As you finish going through each character, have a stage where, with everyone, you recap all of the things that have been decided.

2 Tell the class that one of the characters has a secret which they have never revealed to the other person, even though the characters may have known each other for a long time. In groups of three or four the students now discuss what the secret could be.

3 Bring everyone together again and find out what ideas they came up with. Choose the most popular idea about the secret and make sure everyone is clear on the details (by asking questions and summarising again, as in stage 1).

4 For the next stage, it is also helpful to agree on a 'before, during and after' breakdown of the scene when the secret is revealed. What are the characters doing and talking about before it happened? How is the secret revealed and what happens afterwards?

5 Now, in their groups of three or four again, students can either work with the scenario discussed at stage 3, or go back to their original idea. Ask them to choose two people to improvise the moment when the secret is revealed. The others in the group should watch, direct and provide feedback on how it was done. If they want to they can then swap the roles round.

6 Still working in the same groups, ask them to write up their improvisation as a dialogue between the two characters, remembering to include stage directions as well. Depending on length, it may be more appropriate for them to write up just the most interesting part of their scene. Help them out with their language needs as they do this.
7 Display the dialogues so that they can all be read by the whole class. Which one feels the most like a real scene from a soap opera?

Variation 1

Redistribute the dialogues after stage 6 so that each group has got a different one. Ask them to try out their new script, again with two people observing and two directing. Which dialogue did they prefer working with and why? This process of swapping the scripts around can be repeated several times and is a good way of getting students to provide feedback on each other's work.

Variation 2

Ask the students to learn their scene off by heart for the next lesson. If they wish to, they can then perform them in front of everyone, or for another group. If a camcorder is available, recording the scenes can provide a useful resource for language analysis work later.

Variation 3

Instead of using pictures of only two characters, introduce a range of pictures at stage 1. That way there can be more flexibility in the group work about what the secret could be and about who could reveal it to whom.

7.7 Soundtracks

Outline	Students write and perform a dialogue to go with a piece of background music
Focus	Stimulating creative language use through music
Level	Elementary plus
Time	30 minutes
Materials and preparation	Find a slow, evocative piece of instrumental music which could be used as background music for a film. Samuel Barber's 'Adagio', or Ennio Morricone's theme tune from the film *Cinema Paradiso*, are two good examples. You will also need some other music if you want to use the variation overleaf.

Procedure

1. Tell the class that they are going to hear the background music to a scene in a film in which two people are doing something. As they listen ask them to think about what's happening. Who are the people and where are they? What is the relationship between them? What are they doing? What kind of things might they be saying to each other? Encourage them to make notes if they want to.
2. Ask them to compare and discuss what they imagined with a partner.
3. Get each pair to choose one of the scenarios they imagined, and to develop it into a short written dialogue. Keep the music playing as they discuss ideas and write up what each character is going to say.
4. Students learn their dialogues well enough so that they don't need to look at their papers. They then perform them to the rest of the class, with the music playing in the background. Invite interpretations and feedback from the other students after each dialogue.

Variation

After the students have performed their dialogues with the background music, play some music of a completely different style. Ask them to perform the dialogues to this new piece of music. How does this change the way the dialogues are performed?

7.8 Conscience alley

Outline	Students plan what they might say as advice to someone facing a difficult decision, and then take turns to receive advice themselves from everyone in the group
Focus	Activating language for making future predictions (*You'll probably . . ., I expect you'll . . ., You might . . ., There's a good chance you'll . . . you won't . . . etc.*)
Level	Pre-intermediate plus
Time	20 minutes plus
Materials and preparation	None.

Procedure

1. Tell the class about a course of action where there could be a range of advantages and disadvantages. An example might be going to live in Britain.

2 Divide the class into two sides. One side in favour of the idea, and the other side against it. Ask the students to each write down one sentence which fits in with the opinion of their side. Go round and help out with accuracy as they do this. They should write the sentences as if they are pieces of advice to a real person. For example:

   For: Your English will improve really quickly. I expect you'll find it exciting to live in a different place. You'll probably make lots of new friends, etc.

   Against: There's a good chance you'll miss your family. You might not be able to find a job very easily. It'll be very expensive, etc.

3 Tell the students to remember exactly what it says on their pieces of paper.
4 Ask them to stand in two lines facing each other, with those who are in favour of the idea on one side and those against it on the other. There should be a gap between the two lines so that an 'alley' is created.
5 The first pair of students now start to walk slowly down the central alley. As they walk, the students in the lines say their advice to them. When they reach the end of the alley they rejoin their line and the next pair at the other end start walking down.
6 When everyone has had a chance to walk down the alley, ask the students to sit down again and to discuss with a partner which of the arguments they remember and whether they would make the decision to stay or to go.

Note

This activity comes from the work of the drama in education specialist Dorothy Heathcote. For details of her published work see the book by Betty Wagner listed in the Further Reading section.

Variation

This activity also works well as a way of exploring literature. The 'Conscience Alley' can be set up whenever a character in a story is faced with a difficult decision (for instance Oliver Twist's dilemma of whether to run away or not). Students then go on to read the relevant section, and find out what actually happens.

7.9 From depiction to dialogue

Outline	Students build a dialogue onto a mimed scene from a book they have been reading. This activity works best when the class have all read the same graded reader or other book
Focus	Dramatising a story and making it come to life. Forging links between physical action and dialogue
Level	Intermediate plus
Time	40 minutes plus
Materials and preparation	None.

Procedure

1 Working in small groups, students prepare a depiction (a frozen moment of action where each person takes on the role of one of the characters) of a key moment in the story they have been reading.

2 When each group is ready they present their depiction to the rest of the class who interpret what is happening.

3 Now ask the same groups to prepare a second depiction, showing the situation either a minute earlier or a minute later.

4 Ask them to practise moving smoothly between the first and second depictions, so that they can do it very naturally.

5 Now tell the class that each person in the scene should have exactly two lines of dialogue between the first and second depiction. Each line could be quite long, or it could be as short as a single word. After planning who will say what, the students try to incorporate the dialogue into their scene without altering their previous depictions.

6 Each group presents its scene to the rest of the class.

Note

This is a simplified version of an activity I learnt from the drama in education specialist Eileen Pennington. Its strength lies in the way in which the pre-determined physical action makes the dialogue come across as very natural and flowing.

Variation

Instead of focusing on a scene from a book that the class have all read, use one from internationally known fairytales like 'Little Red Riding Hood' or 'Cinderella'.

7.10 Semi-planned roleplay

Outline Students plan, perform and then reflect on a roleplay situation, in terms of the language used

Focus Raising awareness through dialogue, about specific language items which could be used in a particular situation

Level Pre-intermediate plus

Time 30 minutes

Materials and preparation Decide on a dialogue which your students might realistically find themselves having in English (for one intermediate group who were mostly working or looking for work in Britain, I chose 'Asking your boss for the next day off'). Think of some sentence heads which might naturally be used in this situation. For Example:

Would it be alright if I . . . ?
Is there any chance that . . . ?
Could you tell me . . . ?
To be honest . . .
I don't mind if . . .
I'm afraid . . .
As long as . . .

Procedure

1 Explain to the class what the situation is, and ask them if anyone has any experience of it. Ask them to discuss in pairs what kind of things might be said. Some of the students (especially if they are used to doing roleplay activities) may want to jump ahead and start acting out the situation. For the moment restrain them from this, as they would be missing out on a useful opportunity to reflect on their own language use and receive different ideas from others.

2 Dictate the sentence heads or write them up on the board. Ask them to come up with ways of completing them for both speakers (boss and employee). Help them out with meaning and form where necessary. For my example, some possibilities might be:

Would it be alright if I didn't come in tomorrow? (employee)
Would it be alright if it was just for the morning? (boss)
Is there any chance that I could have tomorrow off? (employee)
Could you tell me why it's so important? (boss)
Could you tell me why not? (employee)
To be honest it's going to make things really difficult. (boss/employee)
To be honest, I did tell you before. (employee)

I don't mind if I don't get paid. (employee)
I don't mind if it's something important. (boss)
I'm afraid it's not going to be possible. (boss)
As long as I can finish early. (employee)
As long as you're back on Wednesday. (boss)

3 Initiate a feedback session on the possibilities they came up with. You may decide to introduce some of your own ideas if it seems appropriate.
4 Allow them some time individually to try to remember the utterances which they feel will be the most useful.
5 Ask them to form different pairs and improvise the situation. They should make the dialogue as natural as possible, whilst trying to incorporate as much of the planned language as seems appropriate.
6 Ask them to go back to their first partner and discuss which of the utterances they were able to successfully use in their dialogue. Were there others that they could have used as well?

Extension

Ask the learners to repeat stage 5 with a different partner. This can be repeated several times, each time rubbing off more and more of the language on the board and forcing them to commit it to working memory.

7.11 The room talks back

Outline	Students write a dialogue between two objects in the room
Focus	Encouraging creative dialogue writing
Level	Elementary plus
Time	30 minutes
Materials and preparation	None.

Procedure

1 In pairs, students choose two objects in the room in which you are teaching. These could be fairly permanent fixtures of the room (the whiteboard and the blinds) or things which might be there only on that day (one of the students' pens or the rubbish in the waste paper basket). They then write a short dialogue between the two objects as if they could speak, commenting on what has been happening in the classroom, either on that particular day or throughout the course, but from the perspective

of the objects they have chosen. They should not use the names of their items in their dialogues.

2 They then perform their dialogues and the rest of the class have the task of working out who is speaking to whom.

Notes

This activity was inspired by 'If a table could speak . . .' in *Motivating High Level Learners* (1996) by David Cranmer. It is particularly useful to do it at the end of a course as it provides students with another angle from which to reflect on what they have been doing together.

7.12 Into the future

Outline	Students write dialogues about themselves at a particular point in the future
Focus	Encouraging discussion about future expectations, and promoting creative dialogue writing
Level	Pre-intermediate plus
Time	30 minutes plus
Materials and preparation	None.

Procedure

1 Ask the students to discuss in pairs what they think they will be doing at a chosen point in the future (after one, five or ten years, for example).

2 Each pair now plans and scripts a short dialogue between themselves at the chosen future point, imagining that they meet by chance in the street having not seen each other since they were in class together. In the dialogue the students should talk about what they are doing and have been doing with their lives. They should not use each other's names.

3 Display the dialogues around the room and ask the students to read them and to try to work out who the speakers are.

Variation

Instead of in the future, students can be asked to write dialogues imagining they are at a particular age in the past.

8 Communicating

The ability to use language to communicate is something which requires practice. Since dialogue provides the interactive format on which all real communication depends, it is the ideal medium in which communicative language practice can occur.

Activities in previous chapters which have focused on production of language have tended to be interactive, but not necessarily communicative. There is a distinction: in interactive activities, learners are asked to use language which has already been planned and processed, and they are therefore not required to modify their utterances based on what they hear the other person saying. In a communicative activity however, each utterance is contingent on what has gone before. That is, learners need to listen to what the other person is saying and respond accordingly. In theatrical terms this can be compared to the difference between rehearsing the lines of a script and taking part in an improvisation.

Of course it is not enough to simply listen to the other person. The speaker needs to understand the words they are using and the listener needs to understand what they are hearing, and it is this need for comprehension that holds the dialogue together. This applies as much to being able to activate a suitable chunk or grammar structure where it is needed, as it does to the ability to pronounce language items so that they are intelligible.

In this chapter dialogue becomes the medium, as opposed to the message. That is, dialogue is less an object to be understood, analysed or created, but rather the means by which information is shared, ideas are communicated, feelings are expressed and reflections are conveyed. The activities here all use dialogue as a way of generating meaningful and communicative interaction between the learners on a one-to-one basis.

Venn diagrams (8.1), Speed dating (8.2) and Gibberish scenes (8.3) look at ways of using dialogue to build and strengthen relationships between students and create good classroom dynamics.

Moving on, Dialogue warm-ups (8.4), The status game (8.5), Cline debates (8.6), Gossip (8.7) and Paper talk (8.8), encourage more extensive, free, spontaneous dialogue and challenge learners to draw deeply on their existing language skills.

Multi-speak dialogues (8.9), ABC dialogues (8.10) and Odds versus evens (8.11) provide some very controlled communication games, and this idea is extended with The yes/no game (8.12), Robinson Crusoe Island (8.13), Who's lying? (8.14), Interclass calls (8.15) and Celebrity ball (8.16) to include more realistic forms of interaction. These activities aim to develop a motivating and memorable context in which particular language areas are naturally activated.

Finally, the last two activities, Boring short stories (8.17) and Read, turn and talk (8.18), look at the active role of the reader in bringing meaning to texts, and illustrate ways in which dialogue can be used to expand and explore written language.

8.1 Venn diagrams

Outline	Students design a Venn diagram to include attributes which are shared and not shared. This activity is most suitable for working with a new group that do not know each other
Focus	Encouraging students to find out information about each other through dialogue
Level	False beginners plus
Time	20 minutes
Materials and preparation	A blank copy of the Venn diagram overleaf for each pair of students (or ask them to draw their own).

Procedure

1 Give out a blank Venn diagram to each pair.

2 Ask them to talk together and to try to fill in several things for each space on the diagram. To do this they need to ask each other questions. At lower levels it's a good idea to model the activity yourself by interviewing one student and filling in a large Venn diagram on the board. Questions could include *Do you like singing? Do you have any brothers and sisters? Can you ski*? etc. At higher levels the students can be encouraged to be more creative in the range of questions they ask. See below for an example.

3 Invite each pair to join another pair. Each pair now introduces themselves to the new pair using the information on their venn Diagrams as a starting point. For example:

I'm Li and this is Maryam. We both learnt to play musical instruments when we were at school. I play the guitar and Maryam plays the piano. Maryam really enjoyed school but I hated it. It was too strict for me . . .

Extension

Display the Venn diagrams around the room in the next class. Ask the students to read them and to try to work out which pair of students wrote each one.

Variation

Instead of working in pairs, put students into groups of three to complete a triple Venn diagram (three interlocking circles).

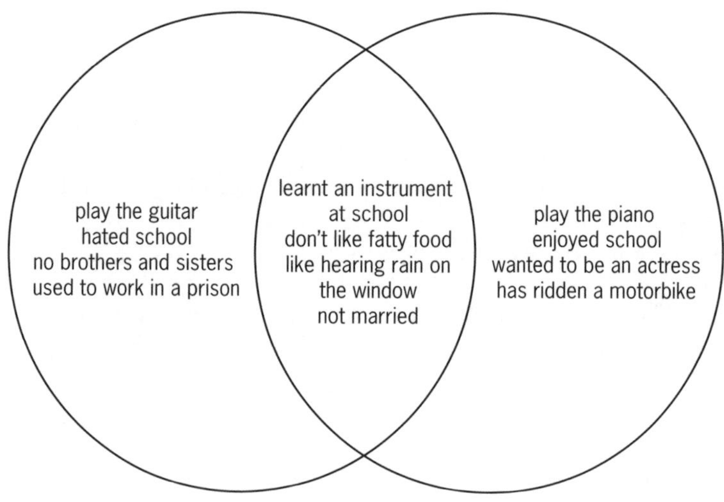

8.2 Speed dating

Outline	Students find out about each other quickly through talking about chosen topics
Focus	Encouraging students to find out about each other through dialogue, and enabling teacher monitoring of speaking ability
Level	Elementary plus
Time	10 minutes
Materials and preparation	Each student will need a copy of a worksheet like the circular 'diagram' on p. 173.

Procedure

1 Invite everyone to stand up in a space where they can move around fairly freely. Give out a copy of the worksheet to each student and ask them to find a partner. Tell them that one of them should choose one of the topics to discuss with their partner but that they will only have one minute to do it in. Emphasise that the interaction should be as equal as possible. Demonstrate this yourself with one student.
2 When a minute is up, give a loud signal for the end of the activity and tell them to swap partners. Each time they swap they should discuss a different topic.
3 When students have interacted with at least three other students, or when you consider it appropriate, ask everyone to sit down. Suggest that they feed back to the person they're sitting next to about who they spoke to and what they found interesting.

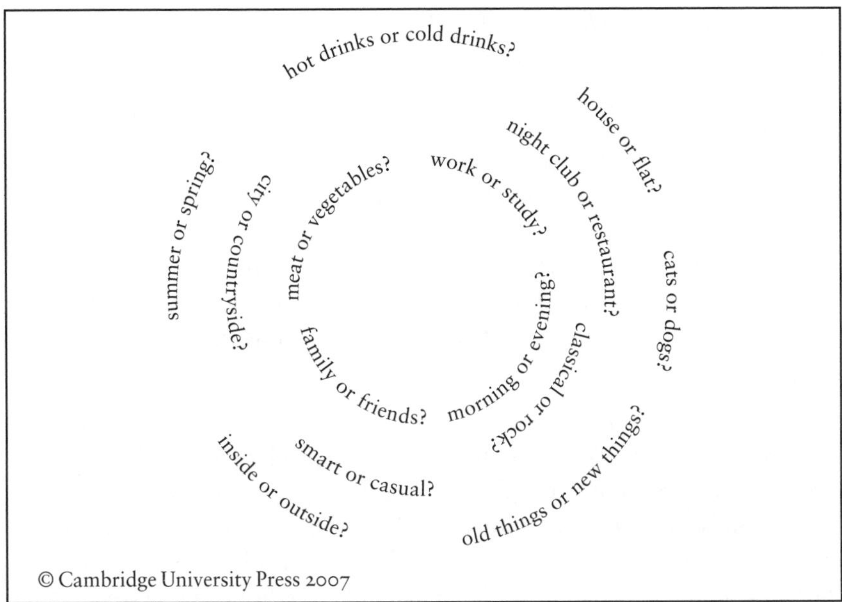

Note

Speed dating has become a popular way for people to meet potential partners. Those who participate in organised schemes are given only a few minutes to introduce themselves and to try to present their positive side. After the allotted time a bell is sounded and everyone moves round to talk to somebody else. At the end of the evening they tell the organisers who it is that they would most like to meet again.

8.3 Gibberish scenes

Outline	Students perform scenes for each other in gibberish (nonsense talk). The students watching have to work out what the situation is
Focus	Emphasising the importance of non-verbal communication and introducing the importance of intonation. Providing practice in interpreting a situation and stimulating laughter
Level	Any
Time	15 minutes
Materials and preparation	None.

Procedure

1 Ask students what languages they can speak. Ask if there's anyone who can speak gibberish. Give them an example (*Blah blah blah-de-blah, blah, blah-de-blah blah* . . . etc.). Try to get a gibberish conversation going with a confident student.

2 With students on their feet and working in groups of three, ask them to prepare to present a short scene to the rest of the group which includes some element of conflict: people disputing the ownership of something, a jealous husband – anything they like. When they speak to each other in the presentation they must use only gibberish.

3 Allow sufficient time for planning but don't let them practise it too many times. Ask them to take turns presenting their improvisations to the rest of the group, who interpret what they think is going on.

Notes

After the students' initial surprise at being asked to speak in a language that is not the one they are learning, this activity can produce a lot of laughter and create a nice classroom atmosphere. It can also be quite satisfying for lower-level learners who struggle to find the right words in English to suddenly be given the freedom to express themselves. With a multi-lingual group, where there is a wide range of different languages, the students can be asked to perform their scenes in their mother tongue instead.

8.4 Dialogue warm-ups

Outline	Students take part in a series of increasingly challenging improvised dialogue activities. These activities can be done one after the other, or as individual activities
Focus	Encouraging free, creative and spontaneous speech
Level	Intermediate plus
Time	5–10 minutes
Materials and preparation	None.

Procedure

1 Organise the students so that they are on their feet (if space allows) and working in pairs.

2 A gives B a topic to talk about for exactly one minute. This topic should not be too easy. If B has been given something about which they know nothing (e.g. sheep farming in Wales) they should talk anyway and invent and be creative. You may need to demonstrate this (and the other stages below) with the students choosing a topic for you first. After one minute swap the roles around.

3 The same as stage 2 but this time A is an alien and knows nothing about this world. A can ask B to explain any word which B uses in their speech. Again swap roles after a minute. For example (the topic is the Antarctic):

B: *In the Antarctic there are lots of wild animals . . .*
A: *What does 'wild' mean?*
B: *'Wild' means not domesticated. So these wild animals have thick fur.*
A: *What's 'thick'?*
B: *I mean long and heavy.*
A: *What is 'and'?*
B: *Well . . . etc.*

4 Student A starts to tell a story. This could be either a traditional story or a personal anecdote. B interrupts A at any point and gets A to adapt what B has just said. A must accept B's interruption and change that part of the story. For example:

A: *Once upon a time there were three little pigs . . .*
B: *No, they weren't pigs.*
A: *Oh no, sorry, they were chickens . . . and they lived with their mother in . . .*

B: *No, it wasn't their mother.*
A: *That's right. They lived with their great uncle . . .*

Variation

For stages 2 and 3, everyone writes their topic on a piece of paper and these go into a hat. Each student now picks one topic from the hat – if they get their own one, too bad!

Note

I learnt these improvisation warm-up activities from Denise Gilfoyle, the director of Up 'n Running Theatre in Birmingham. They are intended to be done as a series of activities one after the other, but also work well as individual exercises.

8.5 The status game

Outline	Students play a game in which they try to work out the status (or level of confidence) which the other students have assumed
Focus	Exploring how language, and other factors, affect the image one projects of oneself. Challenging students to experiment with styles of speaking which they may not normally use
Level	Intermediate plus
Time	20 minute plus
Materials and preparation	Prepare some small slips of paper, each one with a number from one to ten on it. You will need enough of these so that there is one for each student.

Procedure

1 Invite the students to stand up in an area where they can move around freely.

2 Tell them to imagine that ten years have passed since they were last in class together, and that they are all meeting up again at a reunion party. Give each student one of the slips of paper (so that no one else can see it) and ask them to mingle with the other students and to behave and speak according to the status that their slip indicates, i.e. a low number = low status, a high number = high status. You may need to show this yourself first, demonstrating a 1 and a 10 for example.

3 After this has gone on for a few minutes, and everyone's had a chance to chat to several other people, bring everyone together and ask them to say what they think the status of each of the other students is.

4 Discuss what factors helped them to work it out, this may be as much to do with the content of what the learners said (e.g. 'I've just bought a new Rolex watch') as with body language and style of speaking.

Variation

Instead of giving the students a slip with a number, put a sticker with a number on their foreheads, without them seeing the number. This way the students know each other's status but not their own. At stage 2 they work out their own status based on the way the other people speak to them.

Note

In fact, status is subconsciously indicated in numerous ways (position of arms, eye movements, speed and volume of speech etc.) and really has nothing to do with wealth or 'position in society'. Some researchers have suggested that speakers who use the hesitation device *er* a lot tend to be lower in status (*er* meaning *Oh no, I can't think of anything to say!*) than those who use a lot of *em* (*em* meaning *Wait, I'm thinking!*). *Impro: Improvisation and Theatre* (1981) and *Impro for Storytellers* (1989) by Keith Johnstone, contain a wide range of status-type games which can be adapted for use with language students.

8.6 Cline debates

Outline	The class debate controversial statements after positioning themselves in a line
Focus	Encouraging debate and justification of opinions
Level	Pre-intermediate plus
Time	5 minutes plus
Materials and preparation	Choose some statements for discussion which will be appropriate for your group (or use the examples in Box 71 on the topic of the media).

Procedure

1 Ask the class to stand up where there is room for them to position themselves in a line. Explain that you are going to read out some statements and that they should stand in the line according to how much they agree with what you've said. If they stand at one end it means that they totally agree with you, and standing at the other means they totally disagree. Check that they all understand this by standing at various different points in the line yourself, and asking what it means.

2 Read out the statements and allow them time to move into position.
3 Ask them to discuss with the person who is closest to them why they have put themselves there.
4 Encourage some debate between the two extremes of the line.

Box 71

The media

The media shouldn't pry into famous people's private lives.
There should be some control of the media by the government.
Sex and violence shouldn't be shown on TV.
Newspapers should just give us the facts, rather than expressing an opinion.
It should be a crime to make fun of someone's religion in the media.
It should be illegal to have adverts aimed at children.

Note
This activity works well as a way into producing a piece of writing about a particular topic, or to explore the themes of a piece of literature.

8.7 Gossip

Outline	Students develop a story and then spread it as gossip through dialogue with their peers
Focus	Encouraging creative and animated extensive student talk. Promoting retelling and subsequent improvement of a story
Level	Intermediate plus
Time	20–30 minutes
Materials and preparation	Slips of paper with one of the situations from Box 72 (or your own examples) for each pair of students.

Procedure

1 Tell the class a piece of invented news which could have a variety of different reasons for it happening. For example: 'There won't be any school tomorrow'.
2 Ask them to suggest possible reasons why. Take one of their suggestions (or one of your own) and develop it into a story. For example:

'Yes, did you hear . . . they've found a lot of money in a briefcase in the basement and nobody knows where it came from . . . so tomorrow the police are coming to interview all the teachers. It looks like it was stolen 'cos all the notes are brand new.'

3 Give each pair of students a slip with a brief explanation as to why the school is being closed (see the examples below). Ask them to flesh out the details of their story to make it as interesting as possible.
4 Students now mingle, swapping stories with other people. The idea is that they try to convince the others that their story is true by telling it in as animated a way as possible. Encourage them to ask each other questions to get more details.

   If, after hearing a story, they prefer it to their own one, they should use it themselves, and tell it to the next person that they meet.
5 When most people have spoken to each other draw the gossiping stage to a close, and ask the class to feed back to you about which story has become the dominant one.

Box 72

Possible reasons for the school being closed

There's a very contagious disease going round.
The school's gone bankrupt.
There's going to be a hurricane.
The school's going to be turned into a hotel.
One of the teachers has run off with all the school's money.
The school's going to be taken over by the government.
The police suspect there may be a bomb here.
The teachers are on strike.
The government has decided that the building is unsafe.
The heating/air conditioning has broken down.
There have been too many student complaints.
The Director of Studies has been arrested.
There's going to be a surprise party for all the students.

Variation

Instead of speading their stories orally, the students could pass notes to each other around the class to spread their pieces of gossip (see below, Paper talk (8.8)). This is, of course, a way in which gossip is traditionally spread around classrooms (it was in mine at least, when I was a child!) and has the advantage that other learners cannot overhear what isn't being directed at them.

8.8 Paper talk

Outline	Students communicate freely with each other using notes.
Focus	Encouraging written activation of language, through dialogue between students
Level	Any
Time	10 minutes plus
Materials and preparation	A stack of cut up bits of scrap paper, some background music (optional). Arrange the classroom so that students will be able to get up from where they are sitting fairly easily.

Procedure

1 Give out a small stack of slips of paper to each student.

2 Explain that they can communicate with anyone they want to in the class. Ask them to write a short note or a question to somebody. When they have finished they should get up and go over and give their note to that person. This person then replies and the process continues. When everyone's understood what the activity involves, start playing the background music if you have it.

Notes

This activity can be very motivating for students, particularly for those who prefer to express themselves through writing. Eventually you get a situation where everyone is involved in lots of different written conversations at the same time. Sometimes this can mean that the piles of unanswered notes start to build up, and the activity becomes difficult to draw to a close, or carries on into the break.

I first encountered the idea of students passing notes to each other in *The Confidence Book* (1990) by Paul Davis and Mario Rinvolucri.

Variation 1

If everyone can have access to a computer at the same time, then this activity can be done as an email exchange instead.

Variation 2

By taking part in the note writing yourself, you will be able to challenge learners to use particular language items, and provide feedback on what they write to you (see Never-ending dialogue (9.5) in the next chapter).

Variation 3

Instead of getting up and giving the notes to each other, students can communicate in writing with one or both of the students on either side, by simply passing a sheet of paper between them. This way the teacher can monitor the activity, and students are left with a complete dialogue at the end which can be used for language analysis work.

Variation 4

This activity naturally lends itself to practising the language used for talking about particular things (future plans, last weekend, describing where you live etc.) and can of course be set up to do this.

Variation 5

If you want to review language that has previously been focused on in class, write one language item on each slip of paper, before you distribute them at stage 1. The students then need to incorporate the item on the paper into whatever they write on each slip before passing on the note.

8.9 Multi-speak dialogues

Outline	Students take part in a dialogue where questions and answers are built up by each student supplying one word at a time
Focus	Reviewing question formation, with a particular focus on word order
Level	Elementary plus
Time	5–10 minutes
Materials and preparation	None.

Procedure

1 Ask the students to work in groups of four. In each group there are two As and two Bs.

2 Explain that they are going to have a dialogue where the As ask questions and the Bs answer. Each person, however, is only allowed to supply one word at a time (see below). It helps if you demonstrate this yourself first with a few students. You may wish to suggest a topic for the dialogue (*what happened at the weekend*, for instance).

A1: *Where*
A2: *did*
A1: *you*
A2: *go*
A1: *on*
A2: *Saturday?*

B1: *I*
B2: *stayed*
B1: *at*
B2: *home*
B1: *and*
B2: *ate*
B1: *a*
B2: *chicken!*

3 Swap over so that the Bs get a chance to ask the questions.

Notes

Since no one can ever be entirely sure what word their partner is going to say next, this activity is good for developing spontaneity and adaptability on the part of the learners. Because of the way it slows down the process of speech and forces attention to detail, it is also a useful way of raising awareness about the little words (like auxiliary verbs, prepositions and articles) which can otherwise be overlooked.

Variation

Increase the group size so that you have more than two people forming utterances together.

8.10 ABC dialogues

Outline	Students develop a dialogue where each utterance must begin with the letters of the alphabet in order
Focus	Challenging learners to brainstorm possible utterances
Level	Advanced
Time	5–10 minutes
Materials and preparation	None.

Procedure

1 Invite students up on their feet and to work in pairs. Tell them they are going to have a dialogue about whatever they choose but that the first letter of the first word of each person's utterance must be the letters of the alphabet in sequence. For example:

A: *Are you happy being in England?*
B: *Birmingham's really nice, yeah.*

A: *Could you imagine living here forever?*
B: *Don't be ridiculous. I've got to go back to work.*
A: *Ever thought of working here?*
B: *For me it would be difficult . . .*

2 Set them a time limit and see which pair can get furthest in the alphabet. Allow for them to get stuck at times (especially at tricky spots like Q, X and Z!).
3 As an extension, students can be asked to sit down and produce a written version of their dialogue. Surprisingly, they can often remember it really well, perhaps because of the high level of control in this exercise.

Variation 1

Another way of conducting this activity is for the reply to start with the last letter of the previous utterance. So, for example:

A: *Where are you going?*
B: *Germany.*
A: *Yes?. . . Why?*
B: *You know, don't you?*
A: *Unfortunately no, I don't.*
B: *Telling you wouldn't be a good idea.*

Variation 2

Instead of orally, students do the activity in writing by passing a piece of paper back and forth between them. For many students this is slightly easier as it allows more thinking time. The process can then be reversed and students perform their dialogues in front of the class without referring to their sheets. Again, they can usually remember them very well.

Notes

This idea comes from the work of Keith Johnstone. Having to assess the grammatical and lexical appropriacy of each starting word as it is thought of makes this an extremely challenging exercise for students. For more ideas for controlled improvised dialogues suitable for use with advanced level students, see his excellent books *Impro: Improvisation and the Theatre* and *Impro for Storytellers*.

8.11 Odds versus evens

Outline	Students play a game where they need to keep a group dialogue going for as long as possible. This activity is particularly suited to fairly large groups
Focus	Encouraging learners to listen carefully to each other's utterances and to speak clearly
Level	Elementary plus
Time	10 minutes
Materials and preparation	None.

Procedure

1 Go round the class counting the students aloud. Ask them to remember what number they have been given.

2 Now ask all the odd numbers to sit on one side of the classroom, whilst the evens sit on the other. They should sit randomly, rather than in any particular order.

3 The task now is to keep a cohesive dialogue going between the two sides by saying something, and then shouting out the number of the person they want to respond. If they are an 'odd' then they should shout out an even number and vice versa. For example:

1: *Do you like swimming, number 8?*
8: *Yes I love it, number 15.*
15: *Would you like to go swimming after class, number 4?*
4: *Where, number 23?*
23: *In the swimming pool, number 28.*
28: *Is it open, number 19?*
19: *Yes, number 2.*
2: *Are you sure, number 7?*

Each team starts with 20 points. On the board deduct a point from a team if they do any of the following:

- call out a number of someone on their own team
- call out a number which has already been called
- take too long in replying
- change the topic.

4 Each time the dialogue breaks down, students can start again with a new dialogue from a different starting number. The team with most points wins.

8.12 The yes/no game

Outline	Students play a game where they try to avoid saying yes or no
Focus	Encouraging creative language use and exploring alternative responses to questions
Level	Elementary plus
Time	5 minutes plus
Materials and preparation	None.

Procedure

1 Tell the students that they can ask you any question that they want to. Their objective is to try to make you say *yes* or *no*. Your objective is to avoid saying these words.

2 The students ask you their questions. As soon as you say either *yes* or *no* the class is declared the winner.

3 Ask the students to try to recall some of the things you said as responses to their questions. These might include things like *That's right/correct*, and *I do*, *I am* etc. Write up the phrases they remember on the board.

4 Now ask the students to play the game in pairs or threes.

8.13 Robinson Crusoe Island

Outline	Students take part in a pyramid discussion where they need to agree on what items will be useful to them on a desert island
Focus	Building confidence about speaking in bigger groups by starting with dialogue. Activating language for talking about requirements. (See Box 74 below for examples of specific structures)
Level	Pre-intermediate plus
Time	40 minutes
Materials and preparation	Each student will need a copy similar to Box 73 and Box 74.

Procedure

1 Welcome the students as if you don't know them, and congratulate them all on being selected as the finalists to take part in this reality TV show. Tell them that they will all have to live on their own in a remote part of Robinson Crusoe Island in the Pacific Ocean. They are not allowed any contact with anyone else, but can choose eight items from the list below

to take with them. The winner will be the person who carries on for the longest without asking for help or getting ill, and will receive £1,000,000. Give them a copy of the list and ask them to choose individually.

2 When some students have decided what they'll be taking, tell them that you've just been speaking to the programme manager, and that there's been a slight change of plan. Now everyone is going to live on the island in isolated pairs, but each pair will still only be able to choose eight items from the list. They will now have to agree with the person sitting next to them as to what to take.

3 Now tell them that the programme manager has suggested that they all write down what they want to take and why. Give each pair a copy of the sentence heads in Box 74. Elicit an example for each pattern, and then ask them to make sentences for their own ideas.

4 As pairs begin to get their sheets ready, tell them that there has again been a change of plan, and that now they will be living in groups of four and have to agree on a new list. Suggest that they use the ideas that they wrote on their sheets, in the new discussion (or, for an extra challenge, ask them to remember what their sheets said and to turn them over).

5 With classes of up to 20 students, you can keep this process going until eventually you have the whole group working on one joint list. At this stage appoint one student as chairperson, hand them the board pen and ask them to coordinate the discussion.

Box 73

10 boxes of matches
a very sharp strong knife
10 rolls of silver foil
50 books of your choice
a large selection of vegetable seeds for planting
a large barrel of petrol
a spade
a bow and plenty of arrows
a full length mirror
a large piece of tarpaulin (3 square metres)
a radio with a year's supply of batteries
10 thick pads of paper
10 bars of soap
a gas light with 10 spare gas cylinders
a compass
20 pencils
50 fish hooks
20 metres of strong thin thread
20 tins of beans

Box 74

The.....will be useful for....(+ verb...ing)............
We'll need the.........for ....(+ verb...ing)....
If we take the.....we'll be able to ...(+ verb)........
We can use the .... for.........(+ verb...ing)..........
We'll have to take the...... so that we can.......(+ verb)...........

Note

Because of all the dialogue which has gone before, students should be well equipped by stage 5, in terms of confidence and language, to take part in a whole group discussion. This is a useful opportunity for the teacher to take a back seat, observe which students are more dominant, and make a note of language issues. It may also be appropriate to record this stage of the proceedings to be used for analysis later.

8.14 Who's lying?

Outline:	The class interview each other to ascertain whether sentences about other students are true or false
Focus:	Creating a context, developed through dialogue, in which to display and practise language items. This activity can be geared towards any grammatical or lexical focus desired
Level:	Elementary plus
Time:	30 minutes
Materials and preparation	Plan some possible sentences for stage 1 (and for the variation).

Procedure

1 Tell the students three things about yourself which incorporate the language point you are focusing on. For example, to illustrate the experiential aspect of the present perfect, I used:

I've milked quite a few cows in my life.
I've never managed to pass my driving test.
I've eaten snake a couple of times.

Two of the sentences should be true and one false (in my case the last one is false).

2 Ask them to discuss in pairs or small groups which one they think is not true and why.
3 Invite the class to ask you questions to get more information. They can ask you anything they like, but you do not have to answer questions related to the lie truthfully. For example:

S: *Where did you eat snake?*
T: *A few years ago, on holiday.*
S: *What was it like?*
T: *Quite nice really . . . a bit like chicken.*
S: *Was it expensive?*
T: *I'm not sure actually . . . It was in somebody's house.*

4 Ask each student to vote on which sentence they think is incorrect before you reveal the truth.
5 Ask students to write three sentences about themselves in English (one of which is not true).
6 Organise the students into small groups (or do it in plenary if the class is not too big). They take it in turns to read out their sentences whilst the others ask questions to try to work out which sentence is false.

Note

This is a good way of introducing language unobtrusively. By asking questions, students are developing a personalised context within which the target language can be embedded. This is very useful in making the language focus both meaningful and memorable. I first learnt the idea of telling students true or false sentences about the teacher from Paul Davis and Mario Rinvolucri's *Dictation* (1988).

Variation

5 (Stages 1 to 4 as above) Dictate a series of sentences to the class which are about them, and which incorporate the language point you're focusing on. At this stage it doesn't matter whether the sentences are true or false, but they should all be reasonably plausible. Ask the class not to say as yet whether each statement is true or false.

Hye Jun has sung in a choir.
Mahmoud has ridden a motorbike.
Severine has been to Scotland.
Kaori has met a famous person.

Keep going until you've got one sentence each, for about ten of the students.

6 If you feel they need it, suggest that students check their spellings in pairs before writing up the sentences yourself on the board.
7 Ask the students to work individually to tick those sentences which they think are true, and to put a cross against those that they think are not.
8 Students now mingle around and interview each other about the sentences. If something is not true the learner will need to invent the answers to the questions they are asked about it, and be as convincing as possible.
9 When students have had a chance to interview a number of students, conduct a feedback stage where you go through what was true and what wasn't, and find out how well the 'liars' managed to convince the others.

Note

This variation is more challenging in terms of creative and spontaneous student-to-student dialogue on the part of the learners, because it requires the learners to invent the details about a story that they have not come up with themselves. It also allows the teacher to ensure a greater range of examples of the language point being focused on.

8.15 Interclass calls

Outline: The students conduct a survey by telephoning members of another class

Focus: Providing practice in telephoning in English. Encouraging dialogue with students in other classes and providing practice of particular questions

Level: Elementary plus

Time: Up to 90 minutes (depending on the number of students in the classes)

Materials and preparation: A copy of a worksheet like the ones in Boxes 75 and 76 for each student in each class. Students in the first class get worksheet A and those in the second class get worksheet B.

This activity requires cooperation with a teacher of another class (preferably of a similar level) which is scheduled at the same time. Each student will also need a list of the mobile phone numbers of the students in the other class. It doesn't matter if not all of the students have access to a mobile phone.

Procedure

1. Write the names and phone numbers of the students in the other class on the board.
2. Give a copy of the worksheet to every student (those in your class get Worksheet A and those in the other class get Worksheet B). Explain that between them they need to ask all of the questions to all of the students in the other class and note down the answers. The students in the other class will also ask questions to the students in your class.
3. Each student in your class now phones up another student in the other class, asking them all the questions on the list. The student making the call needs to remember to write down the answers. Of course, if someone is already on the phone it will be engaged and they'll need to try dialling someone else's number until they manage to get through. Students who don't have a mobile will need to be interviewed on someone else's phone.
4. When all of the students in the other class have been interviewed, explain that they now need to put all of their answers together. Of course you may also need to wait for the students in the other class to finish interviewing your students.
5. Allocate one question to each of the students in the class. If you have more students than questions then more than one student can work on the same question. Ask them to go around the room collecting all the answers for that question from everybody else in the room.
6. Each student now transforms the information they have gathered into a pie chart which illustrates the information gathered about the students in the other class.
7. All the pie charts are now put together as a poster and presented to the other class.

Note

This activity allows you to say at the beginning of the class 'Can you please remember to turn your mobile phones *on*'!

Variation 1

If not enough mobile phones are available, students could conduct stage 2 as homework via land lines. However, they will also need to liaise by phone within their group to make sure that everyone has been interviewed.

Variation 2

Instead of providing students with a worksheet ask them to design their own one, according to what they would like to find out about the other group, or in order to provide practice in a particular area of language.

Variation 3

This activity can also be set up as a competitive race between the men of both classes versus the women of both classes. The men interview all of the men in their group, and then, by phone, interview the men in the other group. Meanwhile the women do the same thing. They need to do it as quickly as they can, and still remain accurate. They then design pie charts for the information collected for all the men (or all the women) put together. Of course, this works best where there is a fairly even split between the numbers of men and women in both classes.

Variation 4

Conduct the activity via text messaging or emailing instead.

Box 75 (For elementary learners)

Worksheet A

1. Do you live in a house or a flat?
2. Do you pay rent or do you own it?
3. How many bedrooms are there?
4. How many people live in your house?
5. Do you have a garden?
6. Do you know your neighbours?
7. Which room in your house do you eat in?
8. Do you live close to this school?
9. How do you come to school?
10. Do you like where you live?

Worksheet B

1. Do you like cooking?
2. Who usually cooks in your house?
3. What do you have for breakfast?
4. Which type of food is your favourite?
5. How often do you eat in restaurants?
6. What's your favourite drink?
7. Do you drink a lot of water?
8. Do you eat meat every day?
9. What's your favourite sandwich?
10. What do you think about English food?

Box 76 (for intermediate learners)

Worksheet A

1 How much time do you spend studying English outside class?
2 How do you feel about studying English compared with other things that you've studied?
3 What do you most enjoy doing in class?
4 What do you find most difficult about learning English?
5 Do you read for pleasure in English?
6 How much do you use English outside the classroom?
7 Do you think that English sounds nice as a language?
8 How do you feel about talking on the phone in English?
9 Do you think that watching TV and films in English helps you a lot?
10 What has helped you to improve your English the most?

Worksheet B

1 Are you planning to carry on studying English for a long time?
2 What do you see yourself doing this time next year?
3 What do you want to have achieved by the time you're sixty?
4 Are you going out tonight or staying at home?
5 Do you think you're going to get married? When?
6 Are you going to do anything interesting in your next holiday? What?
7 Which member of your family do you think you'll see the most of in ten years' time?
8 What's the ideal job you'd like to have in the future?
9 Is there something that you're really looking forward to doing at the moment?
10 Where would you really like to live in the future?

8.16 Celebrity ball

Outline	Students meet each other at a party in the role of celebrities. They then report back on who they met and what was said to them
Focus	Providing a motivating context in which to engage in dialogue and practise the language of reporting what somebody said
Level	Elementary plus
Time:	20 minutes plus
Materials and preparation	None.

Procedure

1. Ask each student to write down the name of a famous person who they know something about.
2. Tell them that they have now become this person and that they will shortly be attending a party where they'll be mixing with a lot of other celebrities. Ask them to think of some things that they could say to the other guests about what they've been doing recently or what they are planning to do in the future.
3. Invite the students to mingle around and to introduce themselves and chat with the other guests.
4. When everyone has met a few people, ask them to sit down again and to tell the person next to them who they met, and what they remember about what each person said to them. Lower levels can be provided with a 'scaffold' to work with (*X told me . . .*, *Y said . . .*, *Z asked me* etc.)

Box 77

The weather
Your pets
An illness you've recently had
Sport
Your last holiday
Your job
Music
What you think about learning English
Something you've recently read
The News
What you think about where you live.

Box 78

excited
nervous
bored
worried
friendly
tired
polite
irritated
enthusiastic
confident
self-conscious

Notes

This activity is a natural context in which to practise the language of reporting what somebody said. At lower levels this could mean focusing on the typical patterns that follow verbs like *said*, *told* and *asked*, or at higher levels introducing the way in which reporting verbs like *suggest*, *deny*, *persuade* and *admit* work in a sentence.

Variation (for intermediate plus)

The context of a party where students mingle and meet each other is one in which a range of language can be practised. For instance, each student can be given a topic which they need to talk about (see Box 77 above) and an adjective (Box 78) which describes how they are feeling at that moment. They keep this information secret from the other students and try to introduce their topic smoothly and naturally into the conversation with the other people who they meet. This may need a demonstration from you at the beginning. As in the main exercise above, when they've all had a chance to speak to several people they sit down and reflect on who they met, what they talked about, and in what manner they behaved.

8.17 Boring short stories

Outline	The class question short texts to develop more detailed versions of them
Focus	Encouraging students to interact with text in order to enrich it. Language development in question formation. Writing skills
Level	Elementary plus
Time	40 minutes
Materials and preparation	None.

Procedure

1 Put the following short text up on the board or project it on a transparency.

A man walked down the street. *He saw something.*
He picked it up. *He went home.*

2 Discuss with the class what problems there are with this text and how it could be improved.

3 Elicit a list of questions that could be asked about the text in order to get more information. Put them on the board. For example:

What was his name? *Where did he see it?*
Where was the street? *Why did he pick it up?*
What did he see? *How did he feel?*
How did he walk? *Why did he go home?*
Why did he walk down the street?

4 In turn, ask the students the questions (one question per student). Allow them sufficient thinking time and encourage creativity.

5 Ask them to work in pairs and to try to reconstruct the new text which has emerged from the questioning stage.

6 Appoint a class scribe to write a version of the text on the board.
7 Show them the second text or write it on the board.

A woman went out of her house. *She met someone.*
They spoke to each other. *They went inside.*

8 Ask them to work in pairs and to write a list of as many questions as they can think of for this text.
9 Put pairs together and tell them to ask each other their questions.
10 Ask them to write the new story that has emerged.
11 Display the stories around the room and ask the students to discuss the most interesting ones.

8.18 Read, turn and talk

Outline	A very simple activity. As students finish whatever texts they are reading they turn to their partner and discuss what they remember about it and their reactions to it
Focus	Encouraging a personal response to reading material
Level	Any
Time	A few minutes
Materials and preparation	None.

Variation

Give the students a list of sentence heads to complete about texts that they work with in class. For example, for an intermediate class:

I found it quite . . .
I like the bit where . . .
The most interesting/most difficult/funniest/most worrying/ most surprising part is where . . .
Which bit did you find the most interesting/most difficult . . . ?
I can't believe . . .
I didn't know that . . .
Did you know that . . .?
What do you think about . . .?

After reading, the students complete whichever sentence heads they feel they want to and use these as a starting point for the discussion with their partner.

9 Dialogue as learning

In recent years there has been a greater emphasis on a learner-centred approach to learning languages. Sometimes this has meant that teachers have felt uncomfortable about talking freely with their students because they believe that by doing so they are cutting back on opportunities for student-to-student interaction. Another way of looking at learner-centredness is to place the teacher on an equal footing with the learners, as someone who engages with them in dialogue (as opposed to an outsider who merely controls the proceedings). An approach which takes this viewpoint will allow plenty of opportunities for dialogue between the learners and the teacher, alongside learner-to-learner dialogue, because it acknowledges that interaction between proficient and less proficient speakers can provide a rich source of learning.

Learners generally expect to have a language teacher who is a more advanced speaker than they are themselves, and this difference in level should be exploited as much as possible. If the language teacher's only role is to present new language and to set up student-to-student interaction in order to practise this language, then a valuable opportunity to engage in dialogue with the learners, and thereby both to support and to challenge their language development, is potentially lost.

Teachers, with their advanced language skills, are able to consciously adjust their language as they interact with the learners, bringing more complex or simpler language into play where appropriate. As experienced observers of language acquisition, they are also often more able than the learners at making the best decisions as to what new language can be introduced.

This chapter, like the previous one, focuses on dialogue as spontaneous interaction and information exchange between two interlocutors. However, here the emphasis is on ways to incorporate the teacher (or other more advanced speakers), as an active participant in dialogue with learners. Unlike in previous chapters, where the role of the teacher has been mainly to support the learners in their understanding, analysis and construction of dialogue and dialogues, the focus here shifts from product to process. In other words, the dialogue is viewed less as the product of what has been previously learnt, and more as the process by which learning takes place. Accordingly, the activities in this section target ways in which student-to-teacher interaction may be exploited in the classroom as a source of learning.

The closed question restaurant (9.1), Building a life (9.2) and The dating agency (9.3) all use student-to-teacher interaction as a platform by means of which learners can notice aspects of linguistic form. This is extended in Talk and chalk (9.4) and Never-ending dialogue (9.5) to incorporate more natural chat between learners and teacher. In Would you give your teacher a job? (9.6) and The tourists are coming (9.7) the teacher takes on a role in order to increase the range of language that the learners are exposed to and to encourage more student-initiated talk.

Moving into skills work, Dialogic text building (9.8) and Cooperative storymaking (9.9) explore ways of using learner-to-teacher talk as a springboard for learner-produced texts. We then progress onto a focus on more autonomous learning with Teacher in role (9.10), where teacher–learner dialogue serves as a stimulus to promote reading, and finally Interrupting the tapescript (9.11), Dialogue versus internet (9.12) and Difficult dialogues (9.13), which all look at ways of developing learner strategies for dialogic language learning outside the classroom.

9.1 The closed question restaurant

Outline	The teacher presents a range of food vocabulary through a series of closed questions (i.e. questions to which there is a very limited range of possible answers, such as *yes/no* questions or *either/or* questions)
Focus	Vocabulary development around the theme of food
Level	Beginners
Time	20 minutes
Materials and preparation	A set of coloured pens or sweets. Some pictures of restaurants (optional).

Procedure

1 Using pictures and/or discussion, set the context of restaurants in the most appropriate way possible for your group.

2 Assume the role of waitress/waiter and invite one student to sit at the front with you as a customer.

3 Begin to ask the customer a string of closed questions as a way of providing language input that they can immediately use in their replies. Each time you ask a question, hold up one coloured pen or sweet to represent each of the choices you are offering. As the student makes their

choice give them the appropriate item. (If you're using sweets, make sure the students don't eat them immediately!)

The dialogue might work something like this:

T: *Do you want something to eat or something to drink?* (T mimes if necessary and holds up two different coloured pens)
S: *Something to drink.* (T gives student red pen)
T: *Do you want something hot or something cold?*
S: *Something hot.*
T: *Do you want tea, coffee or chocolate?* (T holds up three pens this time)
S: *Coffee.*
T: *Do you want it with milk or without milk?*
S: *Without milk.*
T: *Do you want it with sugar or without sugar?*

4 The student will end up with a range of different coloured pens. With the whole class together, go back through each item in turn, eliciting what it represents (i.e. something hot, coffee, without milk etc.). Resist the temptation to help them too much at this stage. If they really pool their resources they should be able to remember fairly precisely.
5 If you feel that they are ready for some activation at this stage, then distribute handfuls of pens to pairs of students and encourage them to experiment with their own closed question restaurant dialogues.

Notes

Unlike open questions, which challenge learners to produce language for themselves, closed questions can be a very useful way of providing language input which is immediately accessible to the learners and *scaffolding* (see p. 9) the interaction. As an intermediate learner of Spanish in Chile they were certainly useful for me as a way of acquiring new language. For example, having just had the tank filled at a petrol station, I had the following exchange:

Attendant: *¿Quieres pagar en efectivo o con tarjeta?*
(*Do you want to pay in cash or by card?*)
Me: *En efectivo*
(*In cash.*)

Had I been asked simply *¿Cómo quieres pagar?* (*How do you want to pay?*) I would not have been able to draw the phrase *En efectivo* from my own resources. This is a case where the use of a closed question clearly helped me towards acquiring a new language item.

The following two activities also work around the use of closed questions.

9.2 Building a life

Outline	The teacher asks a series of closed questions (see activity 9.1) about a picture of a character, as a way of providing input for a piece of writing about the person
Focus	Vocabulary development and activation through writing
Level	Elementary to intermediate
Time	30 minutes
Materials and preparation	Choose a picture from a magazine or some other source which shows an elderly person who could have had a variety of life experiences. Decide on a set of closed questions to ask about the person which contain language items that are comprehensible but challenging. See below for an example for an elementary group.

Procedure

1 Show the students the picture.

2 Begin asking the class the closed questions. After you have asked each question choose an individual to answer it. This way everyone is challenged to think about the answer. You are aiming for the student to repeat the part of the question that they think is appropriate. You may need to mime or explain meanings where necessary.

3 When you have finished ask the students to write down individually everything that they can remember about the person.

4 Suggest that they pool their ideas in pairs or small groups.

5 Ask them to write a text about the life story of the person. They should include as much of the information as they can remember from the closed questioning stage but also incorporate their own ideas.

Note

The closed questions in Box 79 do not follow the traditional format which tends to be taught. There are two reasons for this. Firstly, this type of 'intonational' question is common in spoken language and secondly, it provides a model of the form required in the answer without the student having to manipulate it. So, for example:

Teacher: *He went to the local school, or he was sent away to school?*
Student: *He went to the local school.*

rather than,

> *Teacher:* *Did he go to the local school, or was he sent away to school?*
> *Student:* *He **went** to the local school.*

Box 79

1 He was born in a small village, or a big city?
2 He went to the local school, or he was sent away to school?
3 He enjoyed school, or he hated school?
4 When he left school, he joined the army, or he went to university?
5 He fell in love with somebody, or he didn't fall in love with anyone?
6 They got married, or they didn't get married?
7 They were happily married, or they used to row a lot?
8 They had three children, or they didn't have any kids?
9 He worked in a bank, or he was an artist?
10 He enjoyed doing the garden, or he did a lot of sports?
11 He kept on working until he died, or he retired from work?
12 He was quite a religious man, or he didn't believe in God?
13 He was happy in his old age or he was a bit lonely?

9.3 The dating agency

Outline	Students ask each other closed questions as a way of building a description of a person. They then try to find a suitable partner for their person
Focus	Vocabulary development on the topic of 'ways of describing people'.
Level	Intermediate to advanced
Time	30 minutes
Materials and preparation	Decide on a list of closed questions containing descriptive language that will be challenging for your group. The list in Box 80 is for an upper- intermediate group. Find a selection of pictures of people from magazines. You will need one picture for each pair of students.

Procedure

1 Discuss the subject of dating agencies with the students. What are they? What kind of questions are asked there?

2 Tell the class that you are going to develop a character for a dating agency through their questions to you. Place one of the pictures on the board where everyone can see it. Give the list of closed questions to a

confident and competent student. Ask them to read out the questions one at a time to you.

3 Give your answer to each question with reference to the picture on the board. Check that they understand the vocabulary by giving examples which explain the meaning as you go.

Student: *Is he **quite a brave person**, or is he **rather timid**?*
Teacher: *Well, he's rather timid, actually. He gets nervous when he meets new people, and he doesn't like having to go to new places and to do new things.*

Of course, you also have the option of not accepting either of the extremes but going for somewhere in the middle.

Student: *Is she **hip and trendy**, or is she **a bit square**?*
Teacher: *Well I wouldn't say she was square, but then she's not really hip and trendy either. She doesn't necessarily wear the latest fashion all the time, but she does wear quite smart, modern clothes.*

4 Give each pair a picture of a person and the list of closed questions. One student asks the questions (and makes a note of the answers) while the other student answers, thinking about the picture they have in front of them.

5 Give students the task of trying to find an appropriate partner for the person in their picture. They mingle around and tell other learners about the person they have created, using their list of adjectives as a prompt.

Well, my person is quite brave and self-confident. She's not really afraid of anything. She is a bit straight-laced though. There are lots of things that she doesn't approve of . . . etc.

They should leave the pictures on their tables as they do this, so that they are making decisions based on their descriptions, rather than simply on what the person looks like. When they have found the most appropriate match, they exchange pictures.

6 Conduct some feedback on this. Who was most suited to whom? Why?

Variation

Instead of matching picture profile with picture profile, students can also be asked to find a real person in the room who would feel comfortable going on a date with their picture profile person. When students have found a person in the room who agrees to go on a date with their picture profile they then show them the picture that their profile originated from.

Box 80

1 Is s/he **quite a brave person**, or is s/he **rather timid?**
2 Is s/he **quite self confident**, or is s/he **rather self-conscious?**
3 Is s/he **fairly open-minded**, or is she **a bit straight-laced?**
4 Is s/he **fairly conventional**, or is s/he **quite rebellious?**
5 Is s/he **hip and trendy**, or is s/he **a bit square?**
6 Is s/he **quite generous**, or is s/he **a bit on the stingy side?**
7 Is s/he **a bit over-sensitive**, or is s/he **as tough as old nails?**
8 Is s/he **very talkative**, or is s/he **a bit reserved?**
9 Is s/he **quite a tidy person**, or is s/he **rather untidy?**
10 Is s/he **quite calm**, or is s/he **a bit quick tempered?**
11 Is s/he **an enthusiastic person**, or is s/he **a bit of a moaner?**

9.4 Talk and chalk

Outline	Teacher and students engage in scaffolded interaction which centres around a particular language area. See also Community language learning (6.4)
Focus	Developing a personalised context in which to present language
Level	Any
Time	20–30 minutes
Preparation and materials	None (but recording facilities will be needed for the variation).

Procedure

1 Ask some of the students in your class questions which use the language area you wish to work with. Try to develop as chatty a style as possible, where the focus is clearly on what the students are saying, rather than the way in which they are saying it. As they reply, gently reformulate or scaffold as appropriate. A typical sequence might go something like this:

T: *So what happened last night after class? What did you do? Margozata?*
S1: *I been my friend house.*

T: *You went to your friend's house, yeah? What did you do there?*
S1: *My friend cooking Polish food.*
T: *Wow! She cooked a Polish meal for you? Great. Was it nice?*
S1: *Yes – is delicious food my country.*
T: *Brilliant. How about you Ahmed? Did you eat at home?*
S2: *Yes, I eat with my wife, my children.*
T: *So you had a nice dinner at home with your family then . . .?*

2 When you feel it's time for a more explicit language focus, ask the class to try to recall what the people who spoke said. This can be done in pairs or small groups, before having an open-class stage. Elicit more correct versions where they are needed and present a sentence for each person on the board. For example:

I went to my friend's house and had Polish food. It was delicious.
I stayed at home and had dinner with my family.

3 Then, with the examples presented clearly on the board, draw the students' attention to the language area that you want them to notice. There are a number of ways in which you could do this.

a Read out the sentences and ask the students to recall who said which one.

b Rub out the parts to be focused on (in this case the past simple verb forms) and ask the class to supply them again.

c Rub out even more of the boardwork so that only some key words remain. For my example this could be:

friend's house	*Polish food*	*delicious*
home	*dinner*	*family*

Ask the class to try to recall the complete utterances.

d Rub out the boardwork completely. Ask the class to test each other in pairs on what each of the people said.

e Elicit further examples which follow the same pattern and present these on the board:

I went to a restaurant and had a really nice meal.

pub	*a drink*
the cinema	*saw a really good film*

Variations

If you have recording facilities available, record the interaction at stage 1. Then at stage 2 the recording can be played back for students to pick out the language you want them to focus on (or indeed the language which *they* want to focus on).

Alternatively, instead of interviewing the students, ask them to interview you about a particular topic (for example, *what you want to do in the future*). Play back the recording and ask them to identify the language items you used to express your future intentions. Use this as the language to present on the board.

9.5 Never-ending dialogue

Outline	Students and teacher engage in a long-term written conversation
Focus	Providing a motivating context for writing, in which scaffolding may take place
Level	Any
Time	Homework plus a few minutes of class time for the extension activities at stage 3
Materials and preparation	A notebook for each student (or a cassette for the variation).

Procedure

1 Write a question to each student in the first page of their notebooks. Aim to write something which would be motivating for the student to think about, and which is comprehensible yet challenging in terms of language input. Do this in dialogue format.

Nick: *How have you been getting on with finding a new job?*
Parvis:

2 Ask the student to write the next line of the dialogue at home and to hand the notebook in to you the next day.

3 You then continue with the next line of the dialogue. Keep this process going for as long as it seems appropriate. At regular intervals ask students to do some reflective work on what has been written. For example, it is useful to get them to cover the dialogue and try to remember what the next line is, or to make a note of new language items which have come up in the text. The following is an example of the first few days of dialogue with a beginner level student.

Nick: *In your letter you say that you haven't got a wife or sons, but you've got one brother and five sisters. That's a big family! Do they live in England or in Yemen?*

Hassan: *This OK.*
But my family they live in Yemen.
No in England.
But I live in a England.

Nick: *Where do they live in Yemen? In a city or in the countryside? What is Yemen like? Is it a beautiful country?*

Hassan: *Yes They live in yemen in a city yafa – in Yemen likes drink coffee and like go to the sea.*

Nick: *I see – people in Yemen like drinking coffee and going to the sea. But what is Yemen like? Is it a big country? Is it beautiful? Is it very hot? Is it expensive?*

Here is an example from a pre-intermediate learner's notebook, where learner and teacher slip smoothly between focusing on meaning and form.

Yayoi: *. . . I think European dinner (?) style is nice. They use hight table chairs. They have dinner (or breakfast) sitting on the chair. It's good for my foot! I don't need kneel down! My food can relax!*

Nick: *Actually I don't mind sitting on the floor to eat. I just don't like kneeling very much. When you say 'My food can relax' do you mean 'My feet can relax' or 'I can have a relaxing meal'?*
You know, something I did really like about meal times in Japan was that you always fill other people's glasses up, rather than your own. Does that still happen?

Yayoi: *'My foot (feet) can relax' I missed spelling. Of course 'I can have a relaxing meal' when 'my feet can relax'.*
Yes that still happen in Japan! Sometimes people say 'If you pour by yourself, you will get marry late!'. Of course it's joke . . .

Variation

Instead of building a written dialogue, ask the students to record their utterances as voicemail (or onto a cassette/cd which you pass back and forth between you). This brings in another dimension, since it allows for scaffolding and reformulation of pronunciation in addition to vocabulary and grammar, but will of course require that each student, and you, have access to recording or voicemailing facilities.

9.6 Would you give your teacher a job?

Outline	The class, in role as managers of a language school, interview their teacher for a job
Focus	Providing opportunities for student-initiated, higher-status language (see also The status game (8.5)) in student-to-teacher interaction. Language development around the areas of question formation and vocabulary for describing people
Level	Pre-intermediate plus (but see variation)
Time	40 minutes
Materials and preparation	None (or copies of a worksheet for the lower level variation like the one given below).

Procedure

1 Invite the students to discuss, in small groups, teachers they've known who they thought were good at their jobs. You may like to model this activity yourself with an example from your own schooldays.

2 Ask each group to come up with a list of desirable qualities of a good teacher, by completing in as many ways as they can the sentence 'A good teacher is someone who. . .'. Encourage them to think of phrases as well as individual words.

3 Arrange for the students to pool their ideas, either in a whole class format, or with a spokesperson from each group reporting to the next one.

4 Ask the students to think of questions to be asked at an interview which would indicate whether the person being interviewed possessed the qualities on their list.

5 Tell the class that they are the directors of the school where you are and that they are going to conduct an interview with you in the role of a teacher looking for a job. Ask them to discuss how they will manage the interview. You may wish to appoint a chairperson at this stage.

6 Go out of the room and return in role as the interviewee. While you are outside decide on what kind of a role you are going to assume. If you are an experienced teacher with few academic qualifications, then become a highly qualified one with no classroom experience. If you are a larger than life, bubbly sort of teacher, then experiment with being a reserved, nervous one. The point is that the students immediately recognise that they are interviewing somebody who is different from the person who usually stands in front of them. As they ask their questions, make your

replies comprehensible but challenging and reformulate what they've said where appropriate. The example below is from an exchange with a pre-intermediate group taking part in the activity.

S: *What's your interesting? You know, what you like. What's your interesting?*
T: *What am I interested in apart from teaching?*
S: *Yes, what are you interested in apart from teaching?*
T: *Em, I'm interested in sport . . .*

7 When they have finished asking their questions, and they seem to want to draw the interview to a close, leave the room and ask them to discuss whether or not they would want to employ you, and the reasoning behind their decision.
8 When they are ready (they may need to come and get you) come back into the room. The class now inform you whether or not you have been given the job, and how they arrived at their decision.

Variation 1

With lower levels it is useful to give them a list of teacher traits at stage 2. They then discuss which ones they think are very important, not important or not good. See below for some possibilities for a beginners/elementary class.

S/he speaks more than one language
S/he is funny
S/he speaks slowly
S/he speaks quickly
S/he has worked as a teacher for a long time
S/he is patient
S/he does lots of reading in class
S/he does lots of listening in class
S/he gives out lots of homework
S/he is hardworking
S/he is serious
S/he knows a lot about English grammar
S/he doesn't come late
S/he isn't boring
S/he uses a lot of pictures in class
S/he does lots of writing in class
S/he does lots of speaking in class
S/he wears smart clothes

Notes

This activity is particularly useful to do towards the end of a term when, hopefully, students will know you sufficiently well to appreciate the difference between you and the role you are playing. They will also shortly be moving on to a new teacher, and it's beneficial for them to start focusing on what qualities they would like their new teacher to have.

Variation 2

Another situation where students take on a role that has a higher status than that of the teacher is a trial. After reading the newspaper story below the class can be asked to think of questions they would like to ask the couple to assess whether or not they are guilty of any crime. The teacher then takes on the role of one of the parents and the class ask their questions. At the end they negotiate to decide whether or not the parent is guilty and if so what the sentence should be.

Mary and Brian Williams left their two children, ages five and one, asleep in their hotel bedroom in St Petersburg, Florida, while they watched a fireworks display from beside the pool. When Tammy, the five-year-old – who had been woken by the fireworks – was found wandering in the corridor by a member of staff, the police were called and the parents charged with child abuse.

9.7 The tourists are coming

Outline	The students plan and propose a weekend of activities for a group of tourists. The teacher, in the role of someone who has no knowledge of the area, discusses the suitability of each proposal with them
Focus	Providing a situation in which scaffolded interaction between students and teacher may occur, and opportunities for subsequent language analysis
Level	Elementary to advanced
Time	Up to 60 minutes
Materials and preparation	Make copies of a worksheet like the one in Box 81 and have audio recording facilities available.

Procedure

1 Put students into small groups and give them a copy of the worksheet. Give them a time limit to discuss and agree on a programme of activities for the weekend.
2 Each group then appoints a spokesperson to report to the tourists' representative with their proposal for the weekend.
3 Place a table in the centre of the room with a tape recorder set up to record. You need enough space around the table for each group's spokesperson and yourself, to sit around comfortably.
4 Press the 'record' button. Take on the role of the tourist's' representative yourself. Invite each spokesperson to put forward their proposal. Ask questions as they go along to clarify what exactly they suggest doing. Make sure that you are playing the role as if you have no knowledge about the place to be visited, adjusting your own use of English so that it is somewhat above the level of the students but still comprehensible.
5 When the discussion has come to an end, and you have told them which group's proposal you have decided to accept, stop the tape.
6 Play the recording back to the class and ask them to write down any bits of language that they hear that catch their attention. These could be items which they would like to be able to use themselves, or just things that they want to check for meaning or accuracy. Do this yourself at the same time, keeping in mind the level of the students. At lower levels you may need to pause the tape frequently to give the students time to write, but make it clear that this is not a dictation task.
7 Students now work in groups to discuss what they have written down. Clear up any problems or questions that come up, if appropriate, in a plenary session. The first time students do this activity they may not make many notes. In this case focus on some or all of the notes that you made yourself.
8 You may wish to follow this up by getting students to come up with their own examples using the language items focused on.

Variation

At stage 6 it may be more appropriate to get students to shout out 'stop!' to you, so that you can stop the tape each time they have a question or want to check what was said. This has the advantage that the language point is still very well contextualised, but it may be more difficult for less confident students to do this.

Box 81

A group of tourists will be coming here for a weekend. They would like to see something of the city and the surrounding countryside, and have a good time. They are between the ages of 18 and 40. They will be staying in cheap accommodation in the city centre and would like to have a programme of activities arranged for each day. Please decide on some suitable activities. The most interesting proposal will be chosen by the tourist group's representative.

	Morning	Afternoon	Evening
Saturday			
Sunday			

9.8 Dialogic text building

Outline Students write a text based on an interview with the teacher

Focus Encouraging written activation of language which has emerged through student-to-teacher dialogue

Level Any

Time 50 minutes

Materials and preparation Choose a personal topic that you will be able to inform the class about (for instance, your last holiday), and be prepared to answer questions from the students about it. You could also offer a range of topics and ask the class to vote for their favourite one. Alternatively, invite someone else into your lesson for this occasion and ask them to talk to the students instead. You will need sets of different coloured slips of paper (a different colour for each pair or group of three students) and recording facilities plus transparencies (for the alternative procedure).

Procedure

1 Tell the class what the topic is and that later in the lesson they will be asked to produce a text incorporating the information you provide them

with. Write the first sentence of a possible text on the board (e.g. *Fifteen years ago Nick went to Japan to work as an English teacher . . .*). Ask them to work in pairs or small groups to plan some questions that they could ask you about it.

2 Distribute the different coloured slips to the different pairs/groups, a different colour for each group. Ask them to write their questions, one on each slip. Each group appoints a 'postperson' who is responsible for delivering their questions to you. As they complete a question they post it to you. You write your reply under their question, feeding in useful language for them to include in their pieces of writing, and post the note back to them. The different coloured bits of paper help to tell you who posted you what.

3 If you begin to get snowed under with notes, or if you want to provide more of a focus on accuracy, you can send slips back to their authors unanswered if what is written on the paper is not correct. The pairs/groups then need to work together to reformulate what they've written, before returning it to you.

4 When you feel that they're ready, ask them to work together to organise the information on their slips into a piece of writing about the topic. Because they have asked different questions each group's text will be different. There is therefore an intrinsic interest in reading the texts written by the others, and they can be displayed on the classroom walls or passed from group to group.

Note

I learnt this technique from Scott Thornbury.

Alternative procedure, including a listening element

1 As above.

2 Ask the students to appoint one person from each group to ask you the questions and invite these people to the front, to sit as close as possible to the tape recorder with you. With small groups of ten students or less it may be possible to huddle together with the whole class.

3 Start the recorder and begin the questioning stage. Answer their questions as comprehensively as possible, making sure that your language is pitched at a level which is suitably challenging, whilst remaining within their grasp. Try to keep this stage under about five minutes.

4 Invite them back to their seats. Now play back the recording so that they can listen to the interaction again, and ask them to make notes to help them with their piece of writing.

5 Ask them to compare notes in pairs and to produce a written text about the topic, incorporating the information they have gleaned from the questioning and listening stage.

Variation

At stage 5 ask the learners to write up their text on a transparency (if available). These can then be projected onto the board and used for language analysis work.

Notes

The example text below is from a pre-intermediate group who interviewed a guest to the classroom about his recent trip to Georgia. The students' writing skills seemed to be well below their ability to speak, so it is interesting to note how much of the language from the interaction stage the learners have tried to incorporate into their text (though not always entirely successfully). Such language items include, *small country, shares borders with, main religion, European descent, growing economy, high standard of living, great variation of climate*.

> I would like to write to you about Georgia. Georgia is a small country in east EUR. It shares border with Russian, Armunia and Azerbaijan. The population of Georgia is 4.5 million. The main religion is Christian but there are other religion like Islam and Jewes too. Most of people are Eur descent. The economique is grewing but the most people don't have high standard of living. Georgia has great variation of climate.

9.9 Cooperative storymaking

Outline	The teacher tells a story but stops at various points to incorporate suggestions from the class. The students then retell/write the story
Focus	Building students' confidence by accepting their ideas into a story, providing opportunities for reformulation of their utterances and developing listening and speaking or writing skills
Level	Any
Time	15 minutes (or more if the story is written up)
Materials and preparation	None.

Procedure

1 Bring the class as close to you as possible and get them into storytelling mode. Tell them the beginning of a story.

2 As soon as you feel they are involved, stop telling the story yourself and wait for a continuation from one of the students. For example:

T: *Once upon a time there was a very old teacher. One day he woke up and looked out of the window, and do you know what he saw?* (wait for a response from a student)
S: *The mother of law.*
T: *That's right. He saw his mother-in-law. And she was carrying something. What was it?*
S: *A box.*
T: *She was. She was carrying a huge box. She put it down on the path and pulled out . . .*

3 As you feel the story reaching a natural conclusion (don't let it go on too long), bring it to a close. Ask the students to retell the complete story to each other in pairs. Alternatively, ask them to write up the story as they remember it.

Note
The key thing to remember with this activity is to be totally open to the suggestions made by the students and not to have a specific story in mind at the beginning. Sometimes the stories that are developed are brilliant and hilarious.

9.10 Teacher in role

Outline	Through a roleplay incorporating the teacher, the class are encouraged to enter into the situation of a piece of literature
Focus	Creating interest in a story and developing motivation to read it. Providing opportunities for higher-status, student-initiated language
Level	Any (the example overleaf is for a beginners/elementary group)
Materials and preparation	Choose a graded reader suitable to the interests and level of the group, where the situation of the opening scene could be presented through roleplay. This example uses the beginners level story *John Doe* by Antoinette Moses, published by Cambridge University Press, in which a man arrives in a hospital having lost his memory.

Procedure

1 Show the students an enlarged copy of the picture of the doctor and patient on page 5 of the book (see below). Discuss with everyone what the situation is and what might be being said.

2 Elicit from the class ideas for questions which the doctor might be asking the patient and put them up on the board. These might include things like 'What's your name?' and 'Where do you live?'. Many of their utterances may require reformulation from the teacher. For example, 'you first time come here?' might be reformulated and written up as, 'Is this your first time here?' and 'You blod press OK?' may become 'Is your blood pressure OK?

3 Ask the students to try to remember exactly four or five of the utterances on the board.

4 Clean the board and set up the situation of teacher in role. The teacher leaves the room, informing the group that when they return they will be a patient and the students will be doctors.

5 The teacher, in role as a patient, returns and the doctors begin to interview them. The example extracts below are from a beginners group engaged in the activity:

S1: *Come in.*
S2: *Come in.*
T: *Hello. Um . . . is this the hospital?. . . Can I come in?*
S1: *Yeah.*
S4: *Sit down.*
S3: *Can I help you?*
T: *Can I sit here?*
S2: *Here.*
T: *OK . . .*

Gradually it is revealed that the patient is suffering from amnesia:

S1: *Is this your first time here?*
T: *I don't know . . . maybe . . . Is it my first time? Did you see me here before?*
S1: *No.*
T: *No? First time?*
S3: *First time.*
S2: *What's the matter?*
T: *I . . . I can't remember.*
S3: *Maybe psychology problem? Psychology problem?*

The doctors now need to work out a way of dealing with this unexpected situation:

S6: *You don't remember you wife?*
T: *I don't know. Am I married?*
S2: *You want stay here?*
S1: *It's free!*
T: *It's free?*
S3: *Yes . . . OK . . . where you passport? Credit card?*
T: *I haven't got a passport.*
S7: *Passport?*
T: *No.*
S3: *No passport? No paper address? Is big problem.*

6 When the conversation seems to have reached a natural conclusion, explain that the situation they've just enacted is how the reader you are

working with begins, and give out copies of the first chapter for them to read.

7 Discuss with the class whether they would like to carry on with the story to find out what happens.

Note

The teacher in role technique was developed in the field of drama in education, and has been written about extensively by the drama specialists Dorothy Heathcote, Gavin Bolton and Cecily O'Neil. For a more detailed analysis on how this approach can be applied to the teaching of languages see S.M. Kao and C. O'Neill (1998) *Words into Worlds: Learning a Second Language through Process Drama*, Ablex Publishing Corporation.

9.11 Interrupting the tapescript

Outline	The teacher reads a tapescript to the learners, who are encouraged to interrupt to ask for language clarification
Focus	Clarifying meaning in context through student-to-teacher dialogue. Developing the listening strategy of asking for clarification
Level	Any
Time	10 minutes
Materials and preparation	Choose a monologic (only one speaker) tapescript (from your coursebook or from a higher level one), that you could read to students in class, and make copies. It should contain language items that you think they won't know, the meaning of which cannot easily be guessed from context. You will need to be prepared to provide spontaneous explanations to their queries.

Procedure

1 Discuss with the learners any problems which they encounter when having to listen to extended speech in English. Ask them how comfortable they feel about interrupting the speaker to ask about something they don't understand. Do they ever pretend that they have understood in order to be 'polite'? Do they sometimes feel that if they keep listening they'll be able to work out what the bit that they didn't understand meant?

2 Explain that you are going to read the tapescript to them and that, for the purposes of this exercise, you would like them to interrupt you each time they feel they haven't quite grasped the meaning of something. Do not help them too much by miming and providing other visual clues, except

when they ask about the meaning of words. As they interrupt, provide explanations which will clarify meaning for them before continuing with the reading. If the class is a very low level monolingual one, this could be done in their mother tongue.

3 Give out the tapescript. Ask them to read it and circle all the points where you were interrupted.

4 Ask them to compare what they've circled, in pairs, and to discuss meanings.

Variation 1

Instead of reading a tapescript, tell the class an anecdote, making a recording whilst you are speaking. Encourage the learners to interrupt in the same way. After finishing the anecdote play the recorded version back to them, and ask them to make a note of all the language items which were queried. They then discuss meanings in pairs as in stage 4 above.

Variation 2

With monolingual groups, read the original tapescript, substituting the more difficult vocabulary items and chunks with mother tongue equivalents. Then read it again entirely in English and encourage them to ask questions as above. This approach provides more support for students.

Notes

'Blocking vocabulary' (language that learners may not understand but need to, in order to understand the text as a whole) is sometimes pre-taught to learners before they listen to the text. This approach has several potential drawbacks. Firstly, an artificial context needs to be created in order to do this, and secondly, it does not really mirror the way that listening happens in the real world. Allowing students to interact with the text, as in this exercise, develops the skill of asking for clarification if and when it is needed, and provides a much more natural way of helping students out with difficult listening texts.

9.12 Dialogue versus internet

Outline One half of the class interview more advanced speakers to find out cultural information, whilst the others use the internet. They then compare their experiences

Focus Encouraging learners to see the language learning potential of both using the internet and having dialogue with native speakers, and discussing the advantages and disadvantages of both approaches

Level	Intermediate plus
Time	Homework plus 20 minutes in the following lesson
Materials and preparation	Make a copy of a worksheet like the one in Box 82 for each student. This worksheet is designed for students studying in Britain. If you are working in a different teaching context you will need a different set of questions. See the variation for classes in countries where English is not the main language of the community.

Procedure

1 Give each student a copy of a worksheet like the one below. Tell them that their homework is to find the answers to as many questions as they can. One half of the class (preferably those with internet access) are to try to find the answers by using an internet search engine, and the other half by asking people of the community you are teaching in. To find the answers to these particular questions they may need to interview people who are over 40 years old.

Box 82

1 Who were Bill and Ben? Find out as much as you can about them.
2 Who was Hilda Ogden? What was she like?
3 What did it mean to 'sound the all clear'?
4 Who used to use a lot of double-sided sticky tape and sticky-back plastic? Why?
5 Find out as much as you can about the system of money in Britain before decimalisation.
6 What kind of a person was Dennis the Menace? What did he get up to?
7 Why was Margaret Thatcher nicknamed 'Maggie Thatcher the milk snatcher'?
8 Who said 'Never has so much been owed by so many to so few'? What was he talking about?
9 What did it mean to have 'six of the best'?
10 What happened in Britain in the summer of 1976?

2 In the next lesson pair off students from different groups. Encourage them to share what they found out, and also to discuss the pros and cons of both ways of finding out the information in terms of their own language development.

3 Discuss issues brought up at stage 2 with the whole class. Possible points to be made are that, whilst the internet may provide large amounts of

information very quickly, and provide opportunities for extensive reading, talking to someone forces oral production of the language and may incorporate more personal references. Both of these factors may help to make it a more memorable experience.

Box 83

Possible answers

1 Bill and Ben were 'the flowerpot men'. Two characters from a children's television programme in the 1950s in Britain. They didn't use English but spoke in their own made-up language instead.
2 Hilda Ogden was a character in the TV soap opera 'Coronation Street'. She was a bit of a gossip.
3 'Sounding the all clear' meant turning on the siren which marked the end of a bombing raid in the Second World War.
4 *Blue Peter* has been a popular children's television programme since the late 1950s. The presenters often demonstrate things that children could make at home out of simple household items. When showing how things could be stuck together they often used double-sided sticky tape instead of glue to save time. They used sticky-back plastic instead of paint.
5 Before decimalisation in 1971 there were 20 shillings to a pound and 12 pence to a shilling.
6 Dennis the Menace is a character in a children's comic called *The Beano*, which has been going since the 1930s. He is very naughty.
7 Margaret Thatcher was nicknamed 'Maggie Thatcher the milk snatcher' in the 1970s when, as newly-appointed education minister, she withdrew free milk in schools for children.
8 Winston Churchill, the British Prime Minister during the second World War, was referring to the Royal Air Force pilots who defeated the Germans in the Battle of Britain.
9 'Six of the best' meant being hit with a cane (six times) as a punishment by your teacher.
10 The summer of 1976 was very hot and there was a drought in Britain. There was also a plague of greenfly, followed by a plague of ladybirds.

Extension

Ask the class to work in their newly formed pairs to produce an illustrated poster outlining the most interesting information that they found out. These can then be shown to other students.

Variation

For classes taking place in non-English-speaking environments, the students could interview other teachers in the school who are native speakers of English or native speakers of English who live in your community.

Note

This activity was inspired by my 8-year-old son's homework from school in Chile. He was asked to find out *Qual es el animal que barritar?* (*Which animal trumpets?*). We actually didn't find out the answer until the next day when André had gone back to school, but the whole family got talking to a lot of different Chileans through trying to find out, and the dialogue which took place certainly helped to make the word *barritar* very memorable for us all.

9.13 Difficult dialogues

Outline	The class experiment with trying out difficult dialogue situations in different ways
Focus	Developing skills for dealing with difficult dialogue situations. Focusing on appropriate language for such situations through scaffolding and/or an explicit language focus on the board
Level	Pre-intermediate plus
Time	30 minutes plus
Materials and preparation	None.

Procedure

1 Have a brainstorm session about situations where it can be difficult to say things. These might include cancelling a previous arrangement, complaining about something, asking for a pay rise, etc. If the class have real experiences that they feel comfortable sharing with the group then so much the better. Choose one of the situations (or ask them to) that they would like to try out in class. A pre-intermediate group, most of whom had children at school in England, worked with the topic of talking to your child's teacher about a behavioural problem.

2 Divide the class into two groups and assign one of the roles (the parent or the teacher in my example) to each group. Within subgroups of two or three, ask them to discuss and plan what they could say in their role. Help them out with language as they require it.

3 Put the students into new pairs, with one person from each group, and ask them to try out the situation.
4 Take on one of the roles yourself at the front of the class, and invite a student to take on the other. Ask the other learners to observe and reflect on the way in which you and the student deal with the situation. You will need to make it clear that you are not performing in the dialogue as yourself. There are many ways in which you could play your role. For instance you could be very vague and not get to the point about what the problem is, your body language could show that you are not really listening, you could interrupt too readily, be too passive, or alternatively be over critical and start making too many accusations.
5 At a suitable point ask the class to comment on how both characters dealt with the situation. Elicit and discuss alternative ways in which the characters could have acted. This may require a focus on useful language, on the board. Now ask for a volunteer to take on your role and to perform it in an alternative way. You now assume the role of the other character.
6 The process of you changing roles can be repeated several times, so that each time a different problem is examined.

Notes

Roleplay situations are often demonstrated in the classroom using the teacher as a participant with one confident student. The students are then asked to try out the same situation in pairs. Sometimes, as in this activity, doing things the other way round may be a more appropriate way of working, with the pairwork serving as a rehearsal for the bigger challenge of performing with the teacher. Language learners often need to engage in difficult dialogues with more advanced speakers outside the classroom, so it seems logical that sometimes they should be challenged to rehearse and reflect on these occasions inside the classroom too.

This activity is based on Augusto Boal's Forum Theatre. In his original technique the spectators (or *spectactors*, as Boal refers to them) are invited to shout 'Stop!' at any point where they feel that there is a problem with the scene that is unfolding, and to come up and take on one of the roles themselves. For an in-depth analysis of Forum Theatre, and other techniques which can be adapted to the teaching of languages, see his excellent book *Games for Actors and Non-Actors* (1992).

Dialogue Bank A

From the film *Mulholland Drive* by David Lynch

Box 84

Scene 1

Betty begins to explore the apartment. After walking a circle in the living room she passes through the kitchen. She moves down a hallway looking at paintings and posters. She goes into the bedroom. She smiles when she sees the bed which has a huge ornately carved head and foot board. She notices the soiled dress on the floor and she frowns as she looks closer. She stands back up, shrugs and goes into the bathroom which has all the original thirties fixtures and floor to ceiling tiles. As she goes toward the sink she smiles to herself in the mirror above it. Suddenly something catches her eye and she opens the shower stall. There before her is the naked, beautiful dark-haired woman.

BETTY

Oh my!

She quickly closes the shower door.

BETTY (cont'd)

I'm sorry. My Aunt . . . Ruth didn't tell me someone was going to be here. I'm so sorry.

DARK-HAIRED WOMAN

That's okay.

BETTY

I'm Ruth's niece. My name's Betty. I'm sure she told you I was coming.

There's a silence.

DARK-HAIRED WOMAN

There was an accident. I came here.

BETTY

I understand. I saw the dress. I . . . I'm sorry. Are you all right?

There is another silence.

BETTY (cont'd)

What happened?

DARK-HAIRED WOMAN

A car . . . a car accident.

BETTY

Are you okay?

DARK-HAIRED WOMAN

I think so. I was just taking a shower.

BETTY

Oh my god. I'm sorry. I'll let you get back to that. I'm going to get unpacked.

Betty goes to the bathroom door and is closing it when she stops and looks back in.

BETTY (cont'd)

What's your name?

We see a close-up of the dark-haired woman. We see her eyes widen with a kind of fear. She's frantically thinking – searching her mind for an answer.

BETTY (cont'd)

I'm sorry. I'll get out of here and we can talk later.

Box 85

Scene 2

APARTMENT BEDROOM
Betty is unpacking in the bedroom and putting her belongings in the closet and the dresser drawers. Many of her Aunt's things are still there.

CUT TO:

APARTMENT BATHROOM
The dark-haired woman is looking at herself in the mirror. She turns and begins looking around the bathroom at shampoos, cosmetics, until her eyes fall on a poster of Gilda *starring Rita Hayworth.*

CUT TO:

APARTMENT BEDROOM
The bathroom door opens and the dark-haired woman comes out wrapped in a towel. She's drying her hair with another. She and Betty stare at one another.

DARK-HAIRED WOMAN

My name is Rita.

BETTY

Hi . . . do you work with my Aunt?

RITA

No . . . I

BETTY

I . . . I mean . . . I . . . it's none of my business.

RITA

She has pretty red hair . . . she is very kind I think.

BETTY

She sure is. She's letting me stay here while she's working on a movie that's being made in Canada, but I guess you know that. I couldn't afford a place like this in a million years. Unless of course I'm discovered and become a movie star. Of course, I'd rather be known as a great actress than a movie star, but sometimes people end up being both and that is, I guess you'd say, sort of why I came here. I'm sorry, I'm just so excited to be here . . . I mean I just came here from Iowa and now I'm in this dream place. You can imagine how I feel.

RITA

I think I've been hurt.

BETTY

Oh . . .

Betty goes to Rita.

BETTY (cont'd)

Sit down . . .

Betty sits Rita on the bed. She leans down and looks at her head and face.

BETTY (cont'd)

Where were you hurt?

Rita motions to her head above her forehead. Betty looks through her hair and finds her wound which has stopped bleeding but is surrounded by a very large blue black bruising.

BETTY (cont'd)

We should get a doctor.

RITA

No.

BETTY

But, this could be serious.

RITA

No . . . I need to sleep.

BETTY

If you have a concussion you shouldn't sleep.

RITA

It will be okay if I sleep. I need to lie down and sleep.

BETTY

All right, but . . . I'm going to check on you.

Rita lies down and is instantly asleep. Betty leans over her and listens to her breathing. She gets a blanket and drapes it over the beautiful sleeping Rita, then leaves the room.

Dialogue Bank B

Authentic snippets[1]

Box 86

1 A: So you've got naturally pause stop play rewind fast forward.
B: Mhm.
A: Right? So everything is there for you. So all you do is plug that into your TV put it onto play and it will show straight away onto your TV.

A = Electrical shop assistant B = Customer (buying a camcorder)

2 A: It's just four nights you want?
B: Well three or four nights which would allow me . . . You know I'm flexible on that. Allow me to come back on either the Friday or the Saturday you see. I suppose in terms of flying. I mean Cardiff but no one seems to go out of Cardiff. I mean why is that then? I mean it's erm.
A: It's only charter flights.

A = Travel agent B = Customer

3 A: Well as I say one was due back on the third of December and the other on the ninth of December.
B: Right. Okay.
A: Erm but we were closed for sort of about a week. And they don't charge you for Sundays I don't think.

A = Librarian B = Customer

4 A: So you found the clutch was slipping and em and what the condition around the clutch?
B: The er the the pressure plate was knackered cos the springs had gone in it.
A: Yes. Right. Okay.

A = Customer B = Mechanic

[1] From the CANCODE Corpus of Spoken English.

5 A: Doug had erm amputation of his second and third toe two days ago. Erm we've had a good recovery from that. Still a little bit of pain from time to time?

B: Yes. Still still painful occasionally yes. But I'm taking pain relief tablets for that.

A: Good.

A = Nurse B = Patient

---

6 A: Hi. Erm I want to pay this er Visa bill.

B: Right.

A: Er from my current account. Now I also have some sterling. Is it possible to put the sterling into my account here or do I have to go to foreign exchange?

A = Customer B = Bank clerk

---

7 A: Yeah please. And then the erm. Oh where we are? The beef and vegetables . . .

B: Number forty-one yes?

A: . . . with the Worcester Sauce. Yeah. Is that with rice as well?

A = Customer B = Waiter

---

8 A: . . . I'm going to Birmingham. I don't em tomorrow but I'm only going one way. I'm getting a lift back. So is it cheaper to get . . .?

B: Right away? Well . . .

A: Or there's not much in it?

A = Customer (buying a train ticket) B = Train station attendant

---

9 A: What about erm . . . Well the only other you know sort of suggestion I could possibly make is supposing we put in erm Right we we proceed with this hole. I cut this out and we we put the up-stand in as part of the original plan.

B: Mm.

A: And then inside there we bring in with some a thin plywood sheet or something like that. You know wood grain. You know with an ash finish.

A = Tradesperson (fitting a kitchen) B = Customer

10	A:	And upstairs I doubt if there's anything left. (*uses keyboard*) Gone.
	B:	Everything's gone for that?
	A:	So that's it. They're they're they'd just be tickets now that someone didn't buy that brought brought them back and we're trying to sell on now.
		A = Theatre box office worker B = Customer
11	A:	Half a pound of red Cheshire please.
	B:	Oh I haven't got any red Cheshire. I've got mild Cheddar.
	A:	Haven't you? No you won't. Half a pound of Cheddar then.
		A = Customer (buying cheese) B = Shop assistant
12	A:	Er I'd try under D I Y.
	B:	Yeah.
	A:	And that's on the top floor that'll be if we've got anything on it.
		A = Bookshop assistant B = Customer
13	A:	Right. It's got a large lounge corner lounge over looking the crossroads in Grange.
	B:	Uh huh.
	A:	Er then it's got a large double bedroom with a erm a built in wardrobe . . .
		A = Estate agent B = Customer
14	A:	Mm. I mean it it is a post-grad thing and it's sort of a salary. Yeah I mean I get money but just not very much. (*laughs*)
	B:	Do you? I think we should put you down and then we can see how much you can borrow jointly. And I'll work out what you can borrow on your own as well.
	A:	Mm.
		A = Student (applying for a mortgage) B = Mortgage adviser
15	A:	. . . payment after that. Are you wanting to claim Housing Benefit and Council Tax?
	B:	No. Because erm I part own the house with the guy that I live with.
	A:	Right. Right. So you don't want to claim Coun= er Council Tax?
		A = Job Centre receptionist B = Customer

16 A: About four days ago. Any drastic change since you've had it?
B: No. (*pause*) Oh my department needs a letter for the medicines I'm on . . . is that a problem?
A: For the?

A = Doctor B = Patient

---

17 A: Right. Erm and that that was how much did you say sorry?
B: Fifty-eight pounds. That includes full English breakfast and V A T.
A: Right. Erm that's great. Erm do I have to ha= leave a deposit or anything?

A = Hotel receptionist B = Customer

---

18 A: It's all right. Yes erm I'm gonna stay in Plymouth for a couple of days. Erm and I just wondered if I could get some information off you. Erm is there is there a swimming pool or in Plymouth?
B: Yes. Erm the one in the city centre. Where are you staying first of all?
A: Er I haven't decided yet but somewhere in the city centre.

A = Tourist information office receptionist B = Tourist

---

19 A: Right. Any other skills that you feel you've developed from work that would also be useful f= for when you're a student?
B: Hm. No not that I can think of.
A: For example things like you know are you working as part of a team? Are you working on your own? Are you?

A = University lecturer B = Someone applying for a university course

---

20 A: How much do you want off?
B: Ermm. Well I like to keep the top quite long ermm, but I like the back nice and short and the sides nice and short. It's just got a bit, you know, a bit grown out of shape.
A: Too heavy?

A = Hairdresser B = Customer

Dialogue Bank C

Snippets from fairy tales

Box 87

1	A:	It fits!	(Cinderella)
	B:	So you were the one I was dancing with!	
2	A:	I'm on my way to my grandmother's house.	(Little Red Riding Hood)
	B:	Do you know what? I think I know a short cut.	
3	A:	No I will not let you in!	(The Three Little Pigs)
	B:	Right then! I'm going to blow your house down.	
4	A:	I thought you said there was a wolf.	(The Boy Who Cried Wolf)
	B:	There was. But it's gone now.	
5	A:	Mirror, mirror on the wall! Who is the most beautiful person in the world?	(Snow White)
	B:	You are your majesty.	
6	A:	Now, don't forget to be back before 12 o'clock.	(Cinderella)
	B:	I won't.	
7	A:	Someone's been sleeping in my bed.	(Goldilocks and the Three Bears)
	B:	. . . and someone's still in mine!	
8	A:	I challenge you to a race.	(The Tortoise and the Hare)
	B:	You??? I could beat you with my eyes closed.	
9	A:	Why are you working so hard? It's a lovely day. Relax.	(The Cricket and the Ant)
	B:	I'm getting my food ready for the winter. You should be doing the same.	
10	A:	But what big teeth you have!	(Little Red Riding Hood)
	B:	All the better to eat you with!	

Dialogue Bank D

25 Lame jokes

Box 88

	Q	A
1	Q: Why did the man run around his bed?	**A: Because he wanted to catch up on his sleep!**
2	Q: Why did the man take away his doorbell?	**A: To win a no-bell prize!**
3	Q: What kind of person sleeps on a lamp?	**A: A light sleeper!**
4	Q: How do scientists freshen their breath?	**A: With experi-mints!**
5	Q: How is an engaged woman like a telephone?	**A: They both have rings!**
6	Q: What did the lawyer name her daughter?	**A: Sue!**
7	Q: What did the mountain climber name his son?	**A: Cliff!**
8	Q: What did the window say to the baby?	**A: 'Stop crying – I'm the one with the pane!'**
9	Q: What did the policeman say to his stomach?	**A: You're under a vest!**
10	Q: What do binmen eat?	**A: Junk food!**
11	Q: What do footballers and babies have in common?	**A: They both dribble!**
12	Q: What do runners do when they forget something?	**A: They jog their memory!**

13 Q:	What do you call a boy with one foot in the door?	**A: Just-in!**
14 Q:	What do you call a giant with lemons in his ears?	**A: Anything you want – he can't hear you!**
15 Q:	What do you call a hippie's wife?	**A: Mississippi!**
16 Q:	What is a boxer's favourite part of a joke?	**A: The punch line!**
17 Q:	What kind of car does an electrician drive?	**A: A Volts-wagon.**
18 Q:	Which super hero lives in a saucepan?	**A: Souperman!**
19 Q:	What's the difference between a jeweller and a jailer?	**A: The jeweller sells watches and the jailer watches cells!**
20 Q:	Why are hairdressers fast drivers?	**A: Because they know all the short cuts!**
21 Q:	Why couldn't the piano teacher open the door?	**A: He forgot his piano keys!**
22 Q:	Why did a boy take a pencil to bed?	**A: He wanted to draw the curtains!**
23 Q:	Why did the boy bring a ladder to school?	**A: He wanted to go to high school!**
24 Q:	Why was the doctor always angry?	**A: Because she had no patients!**
25 Q:	Why was the scientist's head wet?	**A: Because she had a brainstorm!**

Dialogue Bank E

Situational dialogues

Box 89

On the phone

A: Hello.
B: Hello. Can I speak to Maryam Baig please?
A: This is Maryam Baig speaking.
B: Oh hello. It's Pat Jones here from Waterstones.
A: Oh hello.
B: I'm calling about the book you ordered.

A: Hello.
B: Hiya, is that Sam?
A: Yeah. Hiya Pat. Do you want to speak to Jo?
B: Please.

A: Hi, I'm phoning about the room.
B: Yes.
A: Is it still available?
B: It is, yes. Do you want to come and see it?
A: Yes, please. When would be a good time?
B: Well, I'll be there any time after six.

A: Hello. I'd like to make an appointment with the dentist please.
B: Have you used the dentist here before?
A: Yes I have.
B: OK. When were you thinking of?
A: As soon as possible really.
B: I'm afraid we're pretty much booked up until the end of next week.

In a restaurant

A: Are you ready to order?
B: Yes please. Can I have the lasagne please?
A: OK. Do you want salad or vegetables with that?
B: Salad please.
A: OK. Anything else?
B: Just a glass of water please.
A: Still or sparkling?
B: Sparkling please.

At a train station

A: Hi. Can you tell me what time the next train to London is please?
B: There's one in 5 minutes.
A: OK. Which platform?
B: Platform four.
A: I don't think I'll make it.

In the street

A: Have you got the time please?
B: Yeah, it's just gone five.
A: Cheers.

In a clothes shop

A: Can I help you at all?
B: No, I'm alright. I'm just looking.
A: OK, I'll be over there if you need me.
B: Thanks.

In a bike shop

A: Can I have a look at that bike you had on offer in the window?
B: I'm afraid we haven't got any left.
A: Have you got anything else in a similar price range?
B: Erm, not really. Not at the moment.

In a bar

A: What can I get you?
B: Just a cola please.
A: Do you want ice?
B: Just a bit, yeah.

In a hotel

A: Hello. Have you got a single room available?
B: How many nights?
A: Er, just one.
B: Do you want en suite?
A: Em, I'm not bothered really.
B: I've got one room with a shared bathroom.
A: How much is it please?
B: It's £65 a night, including full English breakfast.

At a language school

A: Excuse me. Have you got any places left in the English classes?
B: Only at low levels. Who's it for?
A: It's for me.
B: No, I'm afraid we're full up at everything from intermediate up. You'll have to come back at the beginning of next term.
A: OK. When is that?
B: Enrolment starts on September 2nd.

In a classroom

A: Do you want to open the window?
B: Yes, it is a bit stuffy.
A: Can you manage?
B: God, it's a bit stiff.

In an interview

A: Em, I think your phone's ringing.
B: Yes. Would you excuse me for one moment please?
A: Of course.

Two friends

A: Your phone's ringing.
B: Alright – hold on a sec.
A: Yeah.

Dialogue Bank F

Dating Agency (from the comedy series *Little Britain*)

Box 90

1 Mr Mann: Hello.
2 Roy: Hello, so how can I help you?
3 Mr Mann: I'm looking to meet a woman with the name of Linda Williams.
4 Roy: Right, so you're looking for a specific person?
5 Mr Mann: No, I'm looking to meet any woman with the name of Linda Williams.
6 Roy: Any particular reason?
7 Mr Mann: I like that name.
8 Roy: Right.
9 Mr Mann: It's not my favourite.
10 Roy: No?
11 Mr Mann: No, my favourite name is Catherine Drew, but at my time of life you can't afford to be too picky. Because as I always say . . .

There follows a very long silence.

12 Roy: Right, Ok. (*picks up a clipboard*) Let's just take down some particulars. What aged woman are you looking to meet?
13 Mr Mann: Oh, really, anybody between the ages of thirty-eight and thirty nine.
14 Roy: Right. Height?
15 Mr Mann: She should have some height, yes.
16 Roy: Hair?
17 Mr Mann: I do prefer it.
18 Roy: No, any particular length?
19 Mr Mann: Oh anything from here (*indicating shoulder length with his hand*) . . . to here. (*his hand doesn't move*)
20 Roy: Right, OK, well I'll just have to look in the file. Oh, I can't see anyone in here, one moment. (*goes to the back of the shop and shouts*) Margaret? Margaret?

There is a long pause. The two men smile politely at each other.

21 Margaret: (*off-stage*) Yes?
22 Roy: There's a gentleman here wants to know if we have any women on file by the name of Linda Williams.
23 Margaret: Oh, we've got a Lindsey Williams.
24 Roy: (*turning to Mr Mann*) We've got a Lindsey Williams.
25 Mr Mann: Absolutely no way.
26 Roy: (*shouts*) Absolutely no way.
27 Margaret: Oh.
28 Roy: Oh.
29 Margaret: There's a Linda Willis.
30 Roy: Oh yes. There's a Linda Willis.
31 Mr Mann: Would she be interested in changing her name?
32 Roy (*shouts*) Would she be interested in changing her name?
33 Margaret: I don't know.
34 Roy: (*turning to Mr Mann*) She doesn't know.
35 Mr Mann: Oh.
36 Roy: Oh.
37 Margaret: Roy, Roy, have you checked the red file? I think there might be a Linda Williams in there.

Roy looks through the red file on his desk and immediately finds the page.

38 Roy: Oh. Oh yes, how funny, we do have a Linda Williams, yes, she's thirty-eight, she's got shoulder length hair, very pretty.

Mr Mann looks non-plussed.

39 Margaret: Well?
40 Roy: Well?
41 Mr Mann: (*pause*) Did I mention she should have a glass eye?
42 Roy: (*shouts*) Margaret? Margaret? . . .

Further reading and resources

Bellot, J. (1586) *Familiar Dialogues.*

Boal, A. (1992) *Games for Actors and Non-Actors*, translated by Adrian Jackson, London: Routledge.

Carter, R. and McCarthy, M. (1997) *Exploring Spoken English*, Cambridge: Cambridge University Press.

Cranmer, D. (1996) *Motivating High Level Learners: Activities for Upper Intermediate and Advanced Learners*, Harlow: Longman.

Davis, P. and Rinvolucri, M. (1988) *Dictation: New Methods, New Possibilities*, Cambridge, Cambridge University Press.

Davis, P. and Rinvolucri, M. (1990) *The Confidence Book*, Harlow: Longman.

Deller, S. and Rinvolucri, M. (2002) *Using the Mother Tongue: Making the Most of the Learner's Language*, London: English Teaching Professional.

Freire, P. [1970] (1993) *Pedagogy of the Oppressed*, Harmondsworth: Penguin.

Graham, C. (1978) *Jazz Chants*, Oxford and New York: Oxford University Press.

Hartley, B. and Viney, P. (1978) *Departures*, Oxford: Oxford University Press.

Holquist, M. [1991] (1994) *Dialogism: Bakhtin and His World*, London: Routledge.

Johnstone, K. (1981) *Impro: Improvisation and the Theatre*, New York: Routledge.

Johnstone, K. (1999) *Impro for Storytellers: Theatresports and the Art of Making Things Happen*, London: Faber.

Jones, K. (1983) *Eight Simulations*, Cambridge: Cambridge University Press.

Kao, S.M. and O'Neill, C. (1998) *Words into Worlds: Learning a Second Language through Process Drama*, Ablex Publishing Corporation.

Kurten, B. (1993) *Dance of the Tiger: A Novel of the Ice Age*, Berkeley, CA: University of California.

Ockenden, M. (1972) *Situational Dialogues*, Harlow: Longman.

Rinvolucri, M. and Davis, P. (1995) *More Grammar Games: Cognitive, Affective and Movement Activities for EFL Students*, Cambridge: Cambridge University Press.

Rinvolucri, M. and Morgan, J. (1983), *Once Upon a Time: Using Stories in the Language Classroom*, Cambridge: Cambridge University Press.
Spaventa, L., Langenheim, L., Melville, M. and Rinvolucri, M. (1980) *Towards the Creative Teaching of English*, London: Allen & Unwin.
Stevick, E. W. (1980) *Teaching Languages: A Way and Ways*, Boston, MA: Heinle & Heinle.
Thornbury, S. (2001) *Uncovering Grammar*, Oxford: Macmillan Heinemann English Language Teaching.
Vygotsky, L. (1978) *Mind in Society*, Cambridge, MA: Harvard University Press.
Wagner, B. J. (2000) *Dorothy Heathcote: Drama as a Learning Medium*, Stoke on Trent: Trentham Books.
Willis, J. and Willis, D. (1988) *The Collins Cobuild English Course*, London: Collins.